The
Free Spirit
PHILOSOPHY

J. Kristen Halley

Copyright © 2020 by J. Kristen Halley .

ISBN-978-1-6485-8825-9

All rights reserved. No part of this book may be reproduced or transmitted in any form or by any means, electronic or mechanical, including photocopying, recording, or by any information storage and retrieval system, without permission in writing from the copyright owner.

The views expressed in this work are solely those of the author and do not necessarily reflect the views of the publisher, and the publisher hereby disclaims any responsibility for them.

Matchstick Literary
1-888-306-8885
orders@matchliterary.com

Message to Reader

Nonfiction writers are responsible for publishing the truth. This book is a composite of two trials told as one story to enhance reader comprehension.

The following contains valuable information that will be lost if misunderstood. This section elaborates on circumstances not disclosed elsewhere herein.

Bad-Backstory

I'm physically disabled. After my first back surgery in Y2K failed, the surgeon performed a fusion in 2003. I've had several surgeries and exhausted my options in Western medicine.

As I was becoming increasingly active and had wellness in view. It took less than a second to change everything. I suffered multiple fractures in my lower spine in 2010 when I fell down the stairs.

This tumble came to an abrupt halt when my head was introduced to a cast-iron rail. Everything went dark shortly after my collision.

Ironically, that's the moment my life began to unravel. I sustained more than a garden-variety concussion. My consciousness went black, yet I wasn't unconscious.

I recall only brief fragments that were surreal. There wasn't anything to suggest consciousness wasn't participating.

It's a condition called a *fugue state*. "The fugue state is a rare, often dissociative, form of amnesia…"according to online sources. Basically, it's a time when"the porch light is on, but no one's home."

Hours passed before my consciousness returned. I awoke in a hospital ER and had no recollection of why I was there. I learned about my activities as if I were being told about another person.

The unending convalescence that ensued became more than I could bear. I was consumed by self-pity and had forgotten how my attitude contributes to my wellness. I was conditioning myself to attract negative energy.

I struggled to accept this set back. A pattern of thinking developed that was self-destructive. I internalized it all and kept asking, "Why me?". After losing weight, I became morbidly obese for a second time.

A constant flow of negativity kept the self-degradation fresh. I felt burdensome to my family, hearing my wife strain to push me in a wheelchair up a mild incline was too much.

Strong emotions disabled my intelligence and hid this philosophy. My old perspective reawakened and seemed like all I ever knew.

Those principles in which I believed enough to build my life around were forgotten. I was miserable and attracting more misfortune in my life.

My inversion table flipped over and pinned me to the ground. Another setback, but this one served as a wakeup call. For days, I prayed, pondered, and cried.

I restored archived materials and resurrected journals until I started believing that my prayers were being heard again.

In truth, my higher power never stopped listening; I stopped talking. There's no good time for silence when you need guidance. I needed more faith and awareness. As my original philosophy slowly resurfaced, it fueled my motivation. I had a reason for hope.

Hope is an abstract concept, a belief that things will improve from their current condition. Awareness of self is the first step in understanding human motive and augmenting faith.

Pandemic

It's challenging to see every day as a gift when you unexpectedly lose fundamental liberties. The greater concern is the reason: a global pandemic. A highly contagious virus and the fallout it will have on modern life. We fear nothing more than uncertainty.

How can we relax when there is the constant threat of a contagious virus? There are no vaccinations, yet it's people who become the biggest threat to people in widespread crises. As desperation is perpetuated over time, people hoard products and resources grow scarce.

The social lock-down is due to the *"Corona virus."* We're currently in a struggle againstCOVID-19. This reminds me of how troublesome times come and go, but it'll never stop the Sun from rising. Every morning it shines a light on the dawn of renewed hope. Only in darkness do we see who shines.

Meaning

I've taken time to secure a few loose ends regarding people who helped guide me through my youth. I wanted to express my gratitude for the influence they had on my life's course. My future wasn't always promising.

Now that I have a degree of satisfaction through all I've learned, I want others to know the blissfulness insight brings.

My father passed in 1999. I made it just in time to say the important things, but I cut it close before he slipped into a coma.

His vital signs responded to the sound of my voice. I felt him squeeze my hand just moments before he left this life. A reflex? Maybe, but I choose to believe it was intentional.

Reason

If you believe things happen for a reason, you'll have times when you must live without one. Some reasons are merely the consequences of our decisions.

Reason exists behind everything, and one explains why I gained weight. I had zero physical activity during my post-surgical convalescence. I burned only the calories needed to keep me alive and consumed higher quantities of empty calories.

As a victim of pain, I justified consuming sugars and fat without caution. Despair gave me a false sense of entitlement. I wanted that which delights me under this premise, but it's faulty thinking.

I rationalized that I need at least one thing I can enjoy. It's not a completely mad theory, except that what pleased me was the biggest thing I needed to change.

Change

Change comes in two forms. Negativity is more pervasive, but positive energy is more potent. The type of change you make is a choice. "Feature all things positive" is solid advice.

Today, it's difficult to imagine a home with little or no drama. The environment in some dwellings is destructive to peaceful cohabitation. Sheltered by this philosophy, our house has become a soft place to land. It wasn't an accident.

Awaken your conscience by owning the consequences of your decision. Most people will never experience the cathartic effect over an inflated sense of pride.

We're part of a universe that responds to feelings. Be grateful for every new day, and choose to feel like you're the best version of you.

You may stumble, but you'll rise again and resume pursuit of happiness as is our constitutional right.

You'll have everything you need, but don't harbor exaggerated expectations. It's about having the right priorities and knowing how to arrange them.

While chance is alive and well, it will always impede upon freewill. Blood is spilled when freedom is threatened. It's a natural thing, and not exclusive to our species. Coyotes are known to chew through their own leg to escape a trap.

Spread the Word

When something genuinely works to improve the quality of life, you don't keep it to yourself. Learning this philosophy makes it compelling, even exciting, to share.

Word-of-mouth inspires others to try it. When it's passed along with enthusiasm, it's received with enthusiasm. This approach to improved living can be customized to fit any lifestyle and is no less compelling. When you see how easy and how well it works for you, pass it forward.

Introduction

A few years ago, my blog at WordPress erupted. This spike was unexpected. I'd done little to promote because I used it to draft articles not yet intended for readers.

It became an invaluable source of insight.

Market Analysis

Every writer hears they should write what they know and find a need that they can remedy. I have found such a necessity, and it involves that which I know.

From November to February, I read comments from thousands of readers. This incidental test marketing returned results indicating these are the answers readers want.

The scale of their response suggests this book will find favor in print. How can I turn my back and remain faithful to this philosophy while this book remains unfinished?

Unfortunate Author

How much traffic does it take to overwhelm the servers managed by WordPress? If they didn't know, they do now. When readers commented about my site's dysfunction, their posts came in batches or groupings.

Poor me, I'm the unfortunate author who has too many readers. I hope this misfortune continues. It's puzzling how so many people happened upon my site.

Why did reader interest increase so rapidly? How could I prepare to manage over 5,000comments left in under four months?

I have a theory:

I elaborated on the article and answered questions. It kept the conversation fresh and the readers talking. There is no better way to spread information than word-of-mouth.

It had a snowball effect, growing bigger and faster. It doesn't take an expert to know that adding mass to velocity creates momentum.

My efforts to keep pace reeked of futility. I couldn't respond to everyone, but I couldn't just walk away. Too many people could have a better life. I would be non compliant with my own philosophy to know something beneficial to others and do nothing with it.

I am obliged to write these words out of compassion. A better life is ahead because this is real. It works so well, it may seem too easy. Don't question if it's working; it's fueled by belief.

Need

When the torrent of readers made landfall, it opened a hole of grand proportions. Their show of gratitude was touching. I noticed that most comments requested more posts. This book is my response.

We're all different, and that isn't lost on me. I won't map the next 6-8 weeks of your life. I can share what I did and how I do it. Design your routine to fit your life.

Answers

Helping others achieve wellness wasn't going to happen on any measurable scale, one reader at a time. This book is my answer to finding answers.

Learn a better way to live your life. I fail in my objective unless you achieve yours. Historically, that works in our favor.

Readers were complimentary, and I was flattered. Readers asked to quote me, and I felt accomplished. Good living isn't magic; it's a simple solution to a basic formula.

Visualize Success

If we see success, we can learn to believe it. No matter what you want, every endeavor begins with thought. The problem occurs when it leads to over thinking. We're notorious for blowing things out of proportion.

In sports and other activities, intuition will take over and knows how to execute the motion to achieve success. Allowing your mind to generate anxiety will impede your ability with excessive tension.

Just think of it like playing catch. We don't think about throwing the ball, yet we rarely miss our target.

Initialize the process of change by becoming better acquainted with possibility. Unless you see something as being plausible, you will fail repeatedly.

Fortunately, I've included enough evidence to satisfy that requisite. You can see it for yourself. I have new skills from using an approach that anyone, even those with physical disabilities, can apply to get similar results.

I've demonstrated many benefits of this philosophy on a timeline that stretches back years. It's your reality until doubt drags you under.

Start by conditioning your mind. It's the central command for everything going on in your body. You have resources in your environment, and an active imagination is helpful.

If you think you lack one, you're the reason why. You've said it so long that you're holding back subconsciously to make that statement true. You're as capable as you can believe.

It's common to study history for patterns that help predict the future. However, the record isn't consistent. It factors into probability because if life were a matter of predetermined fate, free will would be a sham.

Life-Coaching

A new kind of profession has been born and is growing fast. More people are finding that a life-coach is just what they needed to turn the chaos into calm.

Life-coaches have the objective to help you identify goals and develop an actionable plan to achieve them. A good life-coach is purposeful and intent on delivering positive results.

Harvard Business Review reports that "The life coaching industry has become a $1 billion a year industry under the radar…[and] growth is expected [to continue]through 2026."

This book is a collection of concepts merged into philosophy and turned into a tangible product. Like a life coach, it's written with purpose and intent and offers comprehensive instructions for living well.

I will keep it simple because it's the best way to convey critical data and yield the highest reader comprehension.

A single book can change the world with the right content. A life-coach encourages clients to use the power of positive energy, and that's the same premise used here.

Fixate on that which matters most. Many of us need help to identify the difference between what is petty and what merits urgency.

Life-coaches help you traverse the trials you encounter while under their treatment. They center on improving health and strengthening relationships. These are the two primary factors in sustained happiness.

This philosophy will shepherd you toward making positive changes in how you think, believe, and behave. Personal improvements are manifest through an abundance of positive energy.

Positive energy is a forgotten resource, which serves us in many ways: protection, motivation, inspiration, and it can be shared. Love is the most potent kind of energy.

I'll challenge some long-standing beliefs. I encourage you to follow the higher logic as you see it. However, I intend to overwhelm your old ideas with evidence that supports making changes.

Don't let a bias nature diminish your life experience. Can you generate happiness from within? Can you conjure positive emotions at will?

You'll want to know how because it affects what kind of frequency your brain emits. It attracts similar frequencies into your life. It's not a secret; it's the *Law of Attraction*.

"As-If"

I acted like a person who is in pain. That realization led me to discover how it made my back pain worse. My behavior was making it real. I had to replace negatively conditioned responses with new ones designed to reflect a person free of pain.

When in public, I walk with a confident stride, my head up, shoulders back, while telling myself that everyone is attracted to me sexually. That isn't true, but being playful is part of my nature.

Confidence can be learned. This section is about using conditioning to act "as if…". Spend time living in the role. If you can convince your mind to believe your performance, it will incorporate confidence into your personality.

In a world of online transmissions and interactions, many portray themselves as something more. But to what end? Nothing is gained. Confidence is a façade.

Being human is a bittersweet experience. The man who speaks often and loudly about how good he lives is on a mission to convince himself. It's likely the opposite of his description. His world is part reality, and partially delusion.

Step outside yourself. Do you approve of who you see? Are you satisfied with your growth? Are you willing to accept full responsibility for the condition of your life?

You don't need a life amidst opulence. It doesn't secure happiness. What is better than a taste of joy that you can savor?

A day serves up enough stress that we need to learn the skills to manage it. If you could use the services of a professional life-coach, take comfort. You already have all you need.

Preface

This book is the epitome of philosophy, a part of life that's been widely abandoned. As vital as it is, it's a forgotten concept. This book is the most useful guide available for living well, of which I know.

Divine Judgment

Religion in the modern world can be traced back to one place: Babylon. It was the epicenter from which today's major religions sprang. There are similarities from prayer beads, trinity, and even a flood story.

Talking about the Bible can cause instant anxiety. I get it. Who among us would stand up to the judgment of an omnipotent and omnipresententity who knows everything we've ever done?

The Bible predicts people will start doubting a god exists, and "The love of the greater number will cool off." They remember Him to curse for their misfortune or when they need saving from imminent danger.

However, it's not God behind natural disasters and global crises. This world has a different governor. What kind of temptation would it be to Jesus to reject kingship over the great cities of the world if they were not Satan's to offer? It says he is here amidst us, he's angry, knowing his time is short.

It's scary shit.

I wouldn't worship any entity who would pitch sinners into a fiery pit, where he employs his adversary, Satan, to torment human souls.

Science has learned that everything in the material world is a form of energy, inside an energy field. Energy is eternal; it only changes form. However, in the Bible, fire is used to represent complete extermination.

It speaks of a second death in the book of Revelations. I surmise this brings our energy form to an end. What more can we lose?

Is death for a sinner really mean fiery flames will burn them eternally, with no chance of parole? Sinners get death for their wages, says the Apostle Paul.

It's excessively out of balance for a god to render senseless, eternal torture for the wicked actions of an imperfect being with a life expectancy of under a hundred years.

Positive Conditioning

If you don't enjoy situations that require thought, find some new interests that do. Your brain is a muscle and will become weaker, like any other idle muscle. Seek positive conditioning frequently rather than in large quantities.

Your brain needs frequent activity to unlock advanced features and create new brain cells. Cannabis has shown to elicit the release of Endorphin sand Oxytocin, the happy hormones, and stimulate more profound thought.

Mid-Life Crisis?

I'm within a few decades of my life expectancy and find myself reflecting on my experience. What have I done with the time I was given?

The answer to that isn't as important as what I will do. The book of my life has the best content in later chapters.

We've all heard about a phenomenon deemed the "Midlife Crises." As a man ages, he's reminded of his mortality. Is this a real condition or just a reason for a man to be self-indulgent?

Misusing a known affliction to justify a large purchase sounds very man-like. Asking for forgiveness is always easier than asking for permission. It's true about men; we're alike, but we're not all the same.

Celebrate Life

When I die, I want those in my life to celebrate it rather than mourning its loss. I haven't any conscious regrets. I've forgiven the injuries I sustained at various stages of my life. And, with forgiveness, comes amnesty.

The relief I felt sparked a new endeavor. I've tendered forgiveness to anyone who injured me and sought forgiveness from those who deserve an apology. I give my best effort to make amends. I can't force forgiveness, so my intent is sufficient for closure.

Die?

Our bodies were made to last. There is a constant cycle of cell replacement or mitosis. Over a few years, every cell in your body is replaced.

However, the inexplicable part is that with each cycle, we get diminishing returns. The replacement cell isn't as efficient as the cell it replaced. It explains why time has a degenerative effect.

Age is a state of mind, and you hear it often when you cross forty. It doesn't make it untrue. The proof of aging is in your mirror. The wrinkles are more profound and remind you life is finite. It's not something on which you should dwell. That is a direct line to habitual self-degradation.

Pride

Accepting that your way of thinking is wrong may be difficult. It's a matter of pride, or rather, being prideful. Pride in one's self and pride of ownership are healthy forms of pride.

Those who tend to be prideful underestimate the difficulty of a situation. They're using a version of pride synonymous with arrogance.

An arrogant person will abandon logic to defend their position, remaining adamant even when the evidence favors the opposition. Be proud, not prideful.

Happiness

How do you define happiness?

It's a feeling, a composition of similar emotions, like exhilaration, delight, enthusiasm, and cordiality. Frequent symptoms of pleasure lead to a diagnosis of happiness.

Meanwhile, the unwell spend every day running around putting out fires at home and the office. It's a life full of stress and drama.

Somehow, someway, all of this started being accepted. Your kids expect things and throw a tantrum when it's denied. Don't blame kids for how they behave, not when you taught them that their behavior works.

Changing the rules for a day after yelling at them in anger has never worked.

Learning Like a Lady loving Life

I love to be whimsical. As a free spirit, I plan to demonstrate the advantages of my philosophy.

This is a chance to learn a new way to live. You can own the recipe for happiness, but you don't start off a master chef. It's easy to forget an ingredient or two, or we simply cannot understand our own instructions.

This book includes more topics that are consistent with happy living. Your health makes everything else possible, so it edges out relationships, although a long, lonely life would be no life at all.

The Impossible

Mine is the story of a man over fifty, physically disabled, weighed up to three hundred pounds, and has a history of negative conditioning. [*b4]

I managed to increase my desire to turn it around. As a husband and father, it wasn't only about me. On day one, it seems impossible, but if I can get results, it will be even easier for you.

I invented a different approach to health, which evolved into a full-blown philosophy. It has applications in every area that has a critical role in your wellness.

Do you think you would have the courage to manage these changes, only without the continual back pain or limitations from a physical disability?

The Moment

The material world has been molded into here and now. Our beginnings are a mystery, but the future is not fated. Life is about the consequences of our decisions. The future is contingent on today's choices.

There are more than words to the adage, "Live in the moment." Take a moment to experience the world around you.

Reflecting on our mistakes is the best way to avoid repeating them. A better life begins at the moment, this moment. In my travels, I stayed in a fishing village in Costa Rica. They use the term *Pura Vida* as a cordial greeting.

Translating the words verbatim means "pure living/life." For Costa Ricans, it's a term of endearment. One resident told me that they're telling each other to live well, prosper, and stay present in the moment.

We're Part of this World

If your life isn't giving you enough in return, what do you need for the life you desire? You need to answer this question because it determines your new headings.

Unless you are willing to accept what life hands you, how much longer before you begin acting proactively? It's your life, your responsibility, but that isn't a bad thing. Any experience you can visualize can be your reality.

I implore you to be opportunistic. Acquire the skills you need to make positive changes permanent. Center your goals around progress. In controlling the means, you'll have more control over the end.

Smiling

When I visualize people practicing better habits from the words I wrote, I get a warm, euphoric feeling. I don't need gratitude, just knowing is enough.

I'm not motivated by personal profit. I'm driven by my need to do the right thing, but don't be misled. I have a family and a strong ambition to provide for their welfare. Money is a resource. It's a means, not an end, because there's more to being a provider. Time is far more valuable to your children.

Our children learn about things in which they're curious. Nurture an enduring curiosity in them, just don't use the word "learning," and they won't realize they're doing it, especially when often profess a disdain for learning.

Be curious about what makes them curious. We learn about our kids by knowing their interests.

You can alter the dynamics of your relationship for the better if you're patient.

To start, keep it simple; smile more. It has a positive effect on everyone. You can't hold a smile for 10 seconds and remain angry. One or the other has to give.

This simple philosophy will answer many questions. Life is full of possibility. The subtext is "grow in a direction that leads you somewhere you desire."

Forward

I did something for a woman on Linked In that compelled her to express gratitude. I don't remember details, but she offered me a choice between two things: She would give me a free copy of her new book, or she would conduct a free spiritual healing over the phone.

I surmised her beliefs were familiar to the Far East. I thought I understood their teachings at a rudimentary level, but I overestimated myself.

I was expecting some variation of talk-therapy. I started talking about the issues that were troublesome in my life when she called.

She was a patient listener, and I revealed something that I'd been reluctant to tell anyone. It was an "experience" that I can't explain, but it changed me at the core.

She wasn't surprised by the extraordinary details I disclosed. She asked HOW I felt different. I couldn't answer, but I did feel different.

I wasn't looking for more speculation, but that wasn't her response. She confidently declared that I had a *spontaneous Kundalini Awakening*.

That sounded impressive! I was relieved my experience had a name and wasn't unique to me. I wasn't crazy. I could accept her explanation but needed to know more.

Another feature that appeared out of thin-air was a strong attraction for truthfulness. Honesty took on real value for me.

Kundalini Awakening

Around 2:00 AM on May 4th, 2004, I was sleeping in my son's room. I don't remember anything unusual up until the moment an unacquainted feeling disrupted my slumber.

This curious sensation at the crown of my head was growing more intense. The instant my finger touched my scalp, a blast of adrenaline coursed through my body. It traveled down my torso into my extremities, where it dissipated.

During the longest second, I felt like I was being held down by something powerful. I was growing frightened when I couldn't move or speak.

I felt the pressure ease and sat up. I held out my arm and seeing it tremble made it very real.

I surveyed the room carefully but didn't see any sign of another presence or feel threatened. Instead, I felt full of hope.

Holy What?

My research on this didn't last. My need to know the reason abruptly lost momentum and died on the vine. I knew it was real, but it's an enigma that remains unsolved. The improvements in my demeanor are enough.

It's unnatural for me to lose my curiosity over something like this, but research felt increasingly pointless. I turned up some comparisons that took my foot off the peddle.

While it took no effort for me to accept it was an awakened Kundalini, when I learned it's comparable to the Christian belief of being anointed by the Holy Spirit, I lost comfort.

I will not imply that I represent a higher purpose. Yet, I can't deny it if I wish to remain objective. Even a remote possibility cannot be dismissed over personal discomfort.

I do what I feel serves my family, my world, and the greater good. Perhaps, in that way, I am serving God's interests.

It's not always easy to see past the many ironies of life; knowing how to do something, and doing it, can fracture. If you're human, you live with it.

Experience is Best When We Make It

This philosophy delivers on its promises. Anyone can use it for results. It's so damn easy to make it permanent. All the elements to build a better life are in you.

It's time. Let's do this. You can look better and enjoy improved health. It's time to get started building a better version of you.

Chapter One: The Free Spirit Philosophy

I've seen the bottom and have no plans to revisit. Choices today create the consequences you live with tomorrow. Simply, prudent behaviors lead to a better life experience. So often, we lack patience and rush essential decisions.

This philosophy was invented out of necessity and evolved over time. It's founded on belief, logic, freewill, awareness, and more.

Disabled, NOT Unable

These life solutions do more than satisfy my promise. It's been expanded to envelop a broader demographic;it's now about more than physical fitness. It's about wellness and perpetuating a happy lifestyle.

I estimate the number of prospective beneficiaries to be reasonably close to the world's population. It sounds grandiose, but it's more than a guess. I made a statement based on first-hand experience and empirical data.

Human behavior is predictable if you understand the pleasure/pain principle. We will always do more to avoid pain than obtain self-gratification. Both are important in understanding human motive. It's natural to search for easier ways to do difficult tasks.

The high volume of visitors elevated my blog into the spotlight, and I learned a lot from readers themselves. It rose to the top of the major search engines, and a reader said it was featured on Yahoo News. This made it easier to find, and another spike ensued.

Truthfully, I was curious about the reader's comments. They were so flattering, and the articles were first drafts and weren't written very well.

One reader warned if he didn't enjoy the content, the poor grammar would be "too much."

I have a working theory about how this clandestine blog became so popular, although it was grammatically challenged. The content is reliable.

It attracts readers who care about living well. These readers have friends who share many of the same interests, like wellness. It's rudimentary evidence for the Law of Attraction.

"Birds of a feather" and "peas in a pod" are two old adages that also support that similar things share much of the same energy and interests.

First drafts are often in rough form, and readers were willing to overlook glaring grammatical errors in favor of content.

Call it a happy accident or a smaller part of a bigger reason; it's guided by logic and is equally useful for anyone.

The material includes more as the result of various trials and delays. The success I achieved with my transformation is extraordinary, and not limited to only what is visible.

Considering I started at a place I describe as less than zero, it makes for a good model.

Before this went to a publisher, I incorporated my findings from comprehensive research. I kept my experience documented. When the smoke cleared, I had laid essential groundwork for a revolutionary approach to wellness.

Crucial Commodity

Information is the most crucial commodity in the world. The best data is almost a form of currency. It's safe to assume that we agree that a comfortable life is preferred over a complicated one.

Here is the time to ask yourself if you believe a prosperous life is even possible. Do you think you deserve it? Is living well something you profoundly desire? Forget about it, UNLESS you believe change is possible.

We're conditioned for unproductive tendencies in the modern world. We procrastinate and become lackadaisical as a by-product of technological advancements. Since this is so damn easy, most won't find it a problem to keep with it.

These are behaviors that matter to quality living. The evidence is irrefutable, so now's the time to begin your journey to look and feel better.

Build an improved version of yourself by learning to manifest your desired reality at will. This is real and very possible. The catch is that it's only possible if your mind believes it.

We live in an on-demand world where instant gratification comes on tap. Therefore, we have a tunnel vision. It's a distraction that allows opportunities to go unnoticed. Every day is full of treasures unless you allow them to remain undiscovered. Stop spectating and start living.

The right philosophy means learning to create and live inside a healthy perspective, protected by self-awareness. This philosophy has an application in veritably every aspect of wellness.

You will sleep more soundly when you have nothing to lament or unprocessed sorrow to internalize. Studies paint a much different picture when guilt is a burden on the mind—the quality of sleep declines from racing thoughts.

Today, I'm healthy and happy. I will always continue to seek improvement. I have already developed many new skills to articulate data to make it easier to understand.

There is no message if it's misunderstood. This is an important subject matter that is logical and practical. There's a reason behind why it became available right on time.

Words

Words have a formidable effect on how we feel. Words carry more power than most realize. It's the words you use, and how, that will determine your success in living.

Practice is central to the kind of changes that endure. Use the right words, and you inspire, but poorly chosen words provoke everything from disdain to apathy. The way we express ourselves will determine how accurately it's interpreted.

Tone

How we say the words can mean more than the words themselves. Ambiguity causes mixed-messages that confuse communications. Don't be vague if you want to be understood.

Words can have a sub-text or meaning that's misinterpreted. It leads to misunderstandings. Emotions can spiral out of control from the illusion of disagreement.

It happens fast, prepare an exit strategy from this pattern of behavior. Positive, descriptive words help define your new perspective for yourself and others. It's an essential part of your transformation.

You're solely responsible for teaching people how to treat you. If they don't treat you like you wish, tell them what you will and will not accept. Avoid underestimating your self-worth.

Increased understanding of this life emanates from the effort you make to focus on the world around you. Intentionally develop your curiosity because you can have a good experience, to the extent you can imagine it. You can't believe that for which you lack reference.

Perception influences your interpretation and frames your understanding of life. The things that you say and the things you think are the things that matter most to your future.

Are you in the habit of saying things like, "I'm so stupid," and think it's harmless because you don't mean it? But is it? I don't expect it to wreck your day, but over time, resorting to negativity becomes a mindless reflex.

We do it without thinking. Your ears hear it, accept it, and it doesn't matter how you said it. Your mind is ready to believe it, especially after seeing what made you say it.

More Words about Words

The US Government changed official terminology to pamper a fickle population during the chaos of a global war, a deadly pandemic, and a time when the whole world was hungry.

They knew the value of using the right words to influence public opinion. They announced that the Department of War would become the new Department of Defense.

It takes more than the right words. Interpretation primarily comes from how the terms are delivered. Nearly Ninety percent of communication happens through body language, including facial expressions, voice tone, decibel level, and posturing. A person who listens attentively has a considerable advantage.

Try influencing your perception with positive words and condition your body with activity, real and imagined. Changing how you believe involves time and conditioning. Say them loud enough to hear your enthusiasm.

Finishing Sentences

Two mature, intelligent people, standing face-to-face, talking increasingly louder and at the same time is not a pretty picture.

They drown each other out, and neither will stop talking long enough to listen.

If you've been here, then you know that neither of you has any idea what was said, only how. There isn't anything productive happening.

It shows that both parties need to develop the composure and discipline to end participation. This is precisely when the contention should end or be revisited if unsettled.

If you haven't trained yourself to remember this feeling under duress, it won't happen naturally. It's not a time to expect affection.

Remove infidelity, money problems, dishonesty, and insecurity, there isn't much left about which a couple can argue. Welcome to a world that is both a paradise and home to misunderstandings.

Understanding Interruptions

In large part, interruptions are rude. In our culture, find anyone who is not guilty of this form of disruption and report them to authorities as proof of extraterrestrial life. I've finished a few sentences that I didn't start. We're all guilty of interrupting.

Sometimes, we think what we have to say is more important than listening to what's being said. It's a collective behavior in an egocentric culture.

I don't rehearse what I want to say. I listen and respond to what is being said.

Any contribution to the speaker's subject is not destructive. This is the difference between a helpful interruption and an intrusion. Do they facilitate progress in your interaction?

Everyone should be given due respect and allowed to speak freely without interruption. We're all entitled to finish our sentence.

Truthfully about Truth

Lying and deceit are commonplace in today's world. Your ability to cling to the truth is determined by the importance you place on it. Do you see any worth in it? Has the truth ever helped you?

You have heard it said, "The truth will set you free."But, that beckons the question, "How does it set me free, and from whom or what?"

There are no shackles on you, yet the truth frees you from more than you expect. Think of it as a computer hard drive. When you are not truthful, then you have to remember what lies you told and to whom. If you only have to recount what actually happened, think of the space you free up, allowing your brain to run more efficiently.

Truth frees you from suspicion. Not many of us know how it feels when people believe what you say. If you have made a habit of lying, it's been a while for you.

Repetition makes us better at whatever we do, including lying. If you have beaten your conscience into submission, how long has it been dormant?

It doesn't just go away. It's with you until you face it. Your conscience has a central role in permanent change. You will need to bring it out of slumber to assist in your overhaul.

Music is Louder When You Face it

Know the joy of being liberated from guilt by owning your life, the good, the bad, and the accidental. Forgive yourself. Plan a day of amnesty and forgive like it's free.

If they hurt you enough to hold a grudge, they mean something to you. Don't leave words unspoken until it's too late.

Peace-of-Mind

If you've been holding on to ill-will, make peace. Do you really want to leave things unsaid when the opportunity to say it could expire at any moment?

My effort to circumvent future regret will only succeed if I forgive and seek forgiveness. Forgiving yourself is more complicated. It serves no purpose to internalize mistakes.

If you feel remorse, you deserve forgiveness. Many people form a tainted judgment of themselves. They believe they deserve a harsher penance for forgiveness.

I've had my share of apologies to make, and I made a genuine effort as I recognize the need. I try to make amends, then I move on. I hope they accept my sincerest expressions, but it isn't the real point. We forgive others to relieve ourselves of unnecessary emotional burdens.

It may be easier said than done, but it can be done. Isn't that really all you need to know?

New Tactics

When we try and fail, we use different tactics to correct the reason for failure.

It will frequently happen when you start, but it shapes into an experience. Every correction you make is another lesson. Every lesson is another lesson learned. The more you know, the closer you get to understanding and awareness.

The data I acquired during the research phase turned up some remarkable findings. I believe that our species possess dormant abilities. Our brain runs software, so to speak, that keeps our brain performing optimally.

Human Supercomputer

In a universe that eliminates waste, keeps order, and maintains balance, why is there so much unused space within such a prominent organ like the human brain?

This organ harbors the mind or our inner voice and is a supercomputer capable of things we haven't imagined. We don't know what we don't know when it comes to the mind. For what we do know, it's a fraction of what we can expect to learn.

We've acquired extensive knowledge about the brain. We have learned about specialized areas of the brain that perform specific functions.

The brain has two hemispheres that are cross-circuited. For example, the right side of the brain controls the left side of the body. Both sides regulate hormone levels and release neurotransmitters in an elaborate feedback system. They do everything from numbing pain to inciting emotion.

The brain is known for keeping out clutter and prunes areas that outlast their usefulness. It essentially compresses the site of the brain that has been idle into a zip file to archive in the subconscious. This process frees up space and helps the conscious mind run more efficiently.

When part of the brain that manages language skills is active, we can learn multiple languages simultaneously. In Aruba, kids learn up to five different languages through school. An adult would faint at that prospect.

A Single Frame of Film

We're told to be present more than ever today, but what does that mean? The moment is but a single frame on a long reel of your life's film.

It's the instant the future is converted to the past, a snapshot in time. To remain in the moment, one second becomes the next, and we follow this succession. It's being aware of what is happening here and now, and the one who listens well has a significant advantage.

I told someone what she posted on Facebook shows wisdom, and she replied, "While life experiences happened, I paid attention [and learned from them. She kept her eyes open.

It was while staying aware that I've amassed discoveries in preparation to challenge long-standing beliefs. I've tendered information supported by empirical evidence.

I managed positive changes that permanently improved my life under extremely challenging circumstances. What is that worth? Maybe, you don't know yet. Now you will.

Internal Dialogue

There's a dialogue happening inside your head between you and your mind. The nature of this discussion can suddenly turn harmful. You're charged to use all means available to make it positive.

This Internal dialogue has taken your life to develop. It needs positive conditioning. You have issues that need to be processed before you can manage meaningful change.

This is where it all begins. It's a process. At first, your thoughts require governing. Always asking, "How do I feel?" can be tiresome. It gets easier.

Your goal is to retrain your mind to be someone who lives with good fortune. Getting what you want means being more grateful for everything you already have. A short inventory will remind you of your blessings.

Negative energy is stealthy. It'll find its way into your mind. If it does pass through your filters, it's okay. You can't stop it no more than you could stop a bird from landing on your head. You wouldn't allow the bird to build a nest. The moment you notice negativity, usher it to the nearest exit.

Science and the Bible Agree

This book shows conclusive evidence from the area where both science and the Bible agree about how people find happiness and love in this life.

From the effect of both nature and nurture to the wise words of Christ, we internalize far too much negative energy.

Jesus counseled his disciples to live each day separately. He implored them to end needless concerns they harbored for tomorrow when today is sufficient in its own evil.

Sentences that Begin, What-If

Almost every question that begins with "What-if?" should be dismissed. These are questions that beckon stress into your life.

When you hear "what if..." in a sentence, you know that what follows can be answered with rhetoric or silence.

Useless Worry

If your body activated your fight or flight reaction, a threat has been perceived. You don't have time to worry if the worst happens now; you can only act. Worry is almost entirely useless.

How often do the things we worry over happen? When they do, it proves this point. In your entire life, can you think of a single time when worry saved the day?

That would be highly unlikely. Worrying over someone or something specific with such feelings increases the risk of you attracting negative energy into the situation and the probability of it happening.

In the form of stress, excess negative energy poses a significant threat to your wellness.

By significant, I mean that it's more harmful than conditions like hypertension, obesity, diabetes, and, yes, cigarette smoking. There are already too many ways for us to die, why expedite matters with useless worry?

Dread

There's a gremlin who wants your every experience to be troublesome. It wants you in discomfort, dissatisfied, and unhappy because it is your introduction to dread.

Dread wants you to fail. We fail at conventional exercise as dread deepens, and excuses present themselves. When possessed by dread, we invent reasons we cannot do our routine.

If you dread your schedule, change it. Where does it say that it has to be done the same way? I learned the same conventional approach to become a certified trainer(CFT).

Three sets of ten are standard issue training. The problem is our inability to keep it fresh. I often tried and failed.

I couldn't make it a regular part of my lifestyle once I lost my commitment to stay with the program. I get contented with my progress and end the program early.

The results I did achieve never lasted until I replaced conventional methods to weight training with a philosophy for living well.

Missing Mobility

For months after my surgery, I spent my time in bed. It was as exciting in much the same way turning a sign with STOP on one side and SLOW on the other all day for road service crews.

I was entertained by syndicated sitcom reruns on Tivo, soft drinks, and…well, that ends my list. No pity, I own the consequences of my decisions that led me back to pain and obesity.

I could've made changes in my diet to account for my lack of activity. Any disregard for health is poor judgment. I wasn't kind to the future version of me, which is a great perspective to try.

You have your past versions, the current version, and tomorrow's version. The current version decides the type of consequences for the future version. Always ask if he'll be happy with the results of your decision before you make it.

It's not easy to defer gratification unless you see it as a small sacrifice for even greater satisfaction.

Nothing in this world is perfect. A genius can be the biggest fool in a room of people who specialize outside his expertise. Poor judgment was the demise of King Solomon. We all make mistakes. How we internalize them determines whether we respond or react.

Mistakes help to form wisdom, and error gives us experience. Learn from the consequences of other people. Why repeat their behavior when you already know where it leads?

Comfort Is No Friend

It's natural to be reluctant when someone drops something new into your lap that involves significant changes in lifestyle. It seems overwhelming at first until you break it down into smaller components. Comfort isn't always your friend, but this isn't complicated enough for all that.

It can be as simple as playing pretend.

Higher Logic

When philosophy fractures with convention, choose to let the higher logic prevail. This method governs my decision process. Whatever your reason for owning this book, it will only be fulfilled if you are honest. Awareness of your behaviors is how you determine which of them are serving you and which are holding you back.

We became who we are over time. Make it a practice to be your own critique.

It's not meant for you to engage in self-degradation. You are beginning a process that involves recognizing undesirable behaviors and reconditioning them.

TFSP is a process of learning how to think and feel. Only this time, you are learning a different way. That is the only way to get different results.

Body Language

My pain was visible in my body language. I remember the effort I made to teach myself patience when I tried not to show how much I lacked it during one of my child's school shows. The more I began thinking like a patient person, the easier it was.

Taking it a step further, I stopped acting like a man in pain. I've stopped grimacing and groaning every time I move. So far, the results are proving capable.

I walk with confidence, I sit with perfect posture, and I use small things to stimulate muscle growth. It has helped me in ways I am still learning. It's helpful if you have enough self-confidence to be wrong and live.

Why Me?

I recall hearing someone rant over literally nothing. We were together when he started, "Why does everything bad happen to me? My life sucks. It's the same old sh*t. I f*ing hate it… my life."

He doesn't see how his quality of life results from the toxic words spewing from his lips into his subconscious.

His temperament is unstable, and he expresses his unhappiness in a loud voice with tones of hostility, profanity, and grief.

His complaining supplies new reasons to complain. Until he's aware of a connection, he'll continue manifesting misery. When he can own his life, he can hope for change.

The World is Broken

I've learned that perception can be more than reality. There are so many ways we can perceive life. Is the world broken?

That depends on your perception of life. Perhaps, we are looking in the wrong places or from the wrong vantage. Our current view could be hiding the beauty of life. A better perspective could reveal that we were put here to delight and to be delighted. Recreation wasn't meant to be condensed into two days a week. Happiness is short-lived and elusive. A happy life begins with good health but includes other things like surrounding yourself with people you love.

World Peace or World Rest in Peace?

How do we increase the love on a planet that desperately needs it? It could take something extraordinary, like divine intervention.

Many believe the Bible prophesizes the State will turn on organized religion and initiate prophecy. Jesus made several prophecies, and only one remains unfulfilled.

He told his followers,"…Only the father knows the hour of reckoning…There will be great tribulation such as the world has never known, nor will know again…"

Will it bring peace to our world? We've failed to come close. Peculiarly, it's patriotism that stands in opposition to world peace. It feels right to support the nation that provides for us.

What You Don't Know

Without awareness, you don't know what you don't know, and what you don't know can kill you. Try becoming more aware of yourself to start.

Be brutally honest and painfully truthful when you evaluate your relationship with yourself, but don't be unfairly harsh. You've been human nearly your entire life. You'll always make mistakes, but you don't have to punish yourself when you do.

Reader Testimonials

This book became my priority when thousands of readers left comments on my blog site. Third-party validation is how we know we have something valuable.

It's unusual for any author to have thousands of unsolicited reader testimony before their book is in print, but I've amassed thousands that speak favorably of this system.

It's prudent to know how others feel about a product before you buy it. We have a 5-star rating system for that reason. Knowing others are satisfied will make purchasing easier.

What form will this philosophy take in your life? The logic is authentic. The gist of what thousands of reader comments say can be summed up with this example:

"Exactly what I needed. Awesome job writing, bro. Can I quote...? This is just what I have been looking for...Keep posting..."

External reinforcement is the kind of affirmation we all use to strengthen inner confidence. Support from those closest should have the most meaning, but even Jesus was still a carpenter to the people in his hometown.

The reader comments were posted by strangers. They have never heard of me, and freely offered unbiased testimony, uninfluenced by familiarity.

The data acquired may have resulted inadvertently; it's no less accurate. It reveals a need shared by a population so large it is difficult to quantify.

I've authored this book to serve this population the answers they've been pursuing. More people deserve to live better, happier lives, and that is my product.

I understand that chance is part of life, so I want to attract opportunity in positive ways.

Chapter Two: Know the Law…of Attraction

It's good to appreciate everything you love about life and the things that make it possible. The more grateful you feel, the more reasons you'll find to be grateful.

If a genie granted you a wish, for what would you ask? Almost immediately, you start to over think such a big decision. Rather than asking for the thing you want, ask what it is you need to get what you want.

Drawn to It

I believe you are serious about improving the quality of your life, and you've been drawn to this book. You're the reason words appear on this page, so you've no reason to second guess your ability.

Trust me, there isn't a superhero behind these words. I hurt my back, had surgery, then another, I got fat, and it facilitated the necessity for a complete overhaul that ends with me sharing my success. I am disabled, not unable.

Nothing is as it Appears

Strip away the material world, and there would be waves, atoms, and sub-atomic particles whizzing by in every direction. Everything looks solid, but nothing is as it appears. It's made up of tightly packed sub-atomic units of energy called quanta.

Everything in the material world is comprised of energy, including us. Everything originates from the same raw material, and it's all connected. Nothing is independent of the energy field in which we dwell.

Lynne McTaggart, author of many books, including "The Field," speaks in detail about what is happening behind-the-scenes of the known world.

Humans are the only species capable of reason, morality, and a desire for justice. Most importantly, we have love to use, to share, and to receive.

Once you can wrap your mind around being part of something bigger, you will understand that love is shared in the light, and misery perpetuates the darkness. Respect the connection you have with the world and its positive experience.

What kind of frequency are you sending out right now? You can always tell by your mood. It affects signal strength and determines the frequency you transmit. If you feel well, then you are forwarding a positive signal.

Intuition VS. Instinct

I used these words interchangeably before I learned there is actually a big difference.

Intuition is infallible. Intuition occurs before conscious thought, and instincts are limited by individual experience and begin afterthought. Instincts can fail you; intuition will not.

Intuition is the ability to surmise situations instantly and execute physical movements without thought. Instincts are different; they are learned and limited to your experiences and nature.

If it's not working, it's not intuition. If we can gain enlightenment without the need for reasoning, from where does this ability come? How far can we use it, and with what applications?

Emotion

Results are hard to measure when feelings can change dozens, even hundreds, of times during a typical day. It's not always dramatic. You might feel frustrated after spilling coffee on your shirt, and it may elicit a curse word or a groan.

That stain will be there all day, but you'll move on. You may have other moments that challenge your composure, but you can manage a typical day, the same as the day before, and just like you expect tomorrow.

A routine that binds us to the mundane blinds us to a hidden reality. So much is happening beyond our vision.

Results?

If results are slow to come or do not come at all, you must accept that it's something you're doing. It always goes back to how you feel. Your frequency corresponds with your attitude and fluctuates along with it.

Have a strong, positive feeling for what you want to attract. We all have heard heralding tales of people doing impossible things during moments of crisis. It happens so frequently that it is called the Placebo Effect.

What one man can do, so can another. The fight or flight reaction with which most of us are familiar is a moment of stress. It's a normal response to external circumstances that threaten the self.

It's a natural reaction to the right conditions, but when unwarranted, it's harmful. This is the stress with which we live—useless worry.

My Request

The Law of Attraction is real. It's not the theory of attraction, so how do you use it? The first time I tried using it, I wondered why it didn't work. It takes time to build the kind of faith required.

Among the detail, there is much to consider. The irony is that the more you think, the more you doubt. However, visualization is the catalyst for achieving success. Using the best logic I could muster, I discerned the logic to ask for something that leads to advantageous subsequent choices.

I confessed that I don't know what I don't know, and I may think I want something, and lament over my choice in hindsight. I asked for strengthened faith and deferred this decision to my higher power.

My first request became about my second. A Creator knows vastly more about the created. He knows what I want and what I need to get it. I felt a sense of euphoria while making my second request.

This absolute feeling was a gift. It lit the path to show me how to start. When my mind kept going back to thoughts of King Solomon, it felt strange in some weird, but significant, way.

The ancient King doesn't come to mind often. He was the wealthiest man in recorded history and regarded as Israel's wisest king.

As the story goes, God gave him a choice, and he made the best one. Great wisdom will deliver everything we want.

Belief Fuels it

If you don't believe you will get what you requested, you're right. It's your belief that guarantees it. You must bring your mind on board, and it's easier for your mind to accept if it's plausible. Add as much detail to your visualizations as possible.

It may not be easy for some to believe the future holds the promise of a better experience. Learn as I did and expect it with as much faith as you can.

With my first request granted, I've proposed my second. Choosing the same answer as King Solomon. I asked the universe for access to use more of my brain.

I remembered to be specific. I requested a higher capacity for learning quickly and the ability to expose deception instantly. I asked for indefinite growth to come at a safe pace, knowing a thin line separates genius from madness.

With any abstract request, visualization is more important than ever. It's challenging to feel sincere gratitude when your gift isn't tangible. Recognition is so essential to the process.

Results are difficult to measure, especially from within. External feedback is the only real measure that counts.

Core

Playing pretend helps improve your reality. Emulate a person who has what you want and learn to think like he does. Visualize it every day.

Look for opportunities. Play a role when traveling or among strangers. See how well you are at being who you think you want to be.

Who I am at the core isn't subjective. I'll never change the contented person I am and the love I have in me because it makes me stronger.

Labels

Create your own label. Let your conscience reawaken. Remember that uneasy feeling when you behave in a way that conflicts with how you believe? It can get worse, but it can also disappear.

Free yourself from guilt as a dishonest person. You didn't become untruthful yesterday, so don't be surprised that a little patience is needed by you and those you deceived.

Once you've been labeled as untruthful, everything you say will be questioned, if not directly, in thought.

Whether you tell the truth or not no longer matters, doubt will be attached to everything you say. Demonstrating yourself as an honest person takes time. You chose to lie, so you're not the victim.

Chapter Three: The Healthy Self

In eight months, I lost over a hundred and twenty pounds, and I did it without excessive sagging skin. This unfortunate side-effect frequently happens to those experiencing rapid weight loss from surgery, or when weight is lost through diet alone. You wanted to look better, not look like melting ice cream.

Warning!

Before we go further, I'm obligated to warn you this product assumes you can adapt. I'm not a former Navy Seal, but you must measure up against the rigorous lifestyle of a middle-aged man who is physically handicapped from a spinal fusion.

By default, I am conditioned to be lazy. It was already challenging to get started with back pain. I lack mobility, and still, despite every disadvantage, it works.

I saw veins in my body that haven't been close enough to the surface in a long time. I want to be an example of its effectiveness.

Years from now, this book will still be here to remind you of when you did the things that made real changes in your life. I do my best to follow this advice, but as a human, I fail and start over.

This chapter is all about losing a different kind of weight. This weight has been with you for so long, you forget about it.

Life's package comes complete. From Bliss to sadness, the choice is yours to make. A traumatic childhood is becoming the new norm. As you mature, if you've left regrets unchecked, they amass into a heavyweight. This is the baggage you should leave unclaimed.

The difference between living with baggage and sitting it down is like the difference in seeing a beautiful sunset and hearing one.

I have a reason to reach out to those like myself, mature, limited in some way, disabled, and overweight. I also wanted to reach those people who are unhappy. It doesn't have to be that way.

`Govern It, Own It, Change It`

Words are the very foundation of civilization. What would we be without language? What you say and what you think are both choices.

Keeping your mind focused is not easy. You'll need time for learning patience. I feel like I'm telling you to learn Latin. Latin would be easier, except you don't have the patience.

You can change your thinking by governing what you think and say, correcting it when you recognize it, then rephrasing it differently.

You can do all this before any words are said and avert incidental harm. Unfortunately, we save our thinking for the end. How many times have you lamented over how you handled something?

My Secret's no Secret

Your mind doesn't recognize your imagination or distinguish it from reality. You can use this to your advantage and convince your body to stimulate feedback in response to its perceived workload. Anticipation that the current workload will continue elicits feed back to build more endurance and muscle tone.

The mind and the brain are terms often used synonymously. There is a difference. The brain is housed inside your skull and home to the mind, but they're not the same.

The mind transcends the intellect. This explains how we can sense someone is behind us or know we are being watched. Your mind is the conscious life force that is a manifestation of your soul. It's the force within us that communicates innovative ideas or offers up workable solutions to a problem.

Scripting

I've always preferred writing fiction, particularly in screenplay format. There are a few golden rules to know when writing a script.

Every new scene or change of location begins with a Scene Heading. It's in all upper-case and sets the stage. They all start with "EXT," "INT," or "I/E" indicates whether it's inside, outside, or both. Then, go from general to specific. Always end with the time, day, or night.

You're a character, among others, that represent other people in your life. Use Action to describe the scene, site, and activity. The dialogue is crucial because it means the words you should have used or will use. Whether or not it plays out according to script is less important than being present.

It's cathartic beyond description. It's also an excellent method to enlighten awareness. We all have moments we wish we could relive, only better. You're not chained to any script. Improvisation is likely, so flexibility is essential.

Lead Role

Just the other night, I played the role of a pool-shark. People who know me know that I have been a decent player for a while. I never owned a table, and sometimes years have passed between games. I was 50-50 win or lose. That night, someone showed up who looked like me, only he never misses.

I won sixteen consecutive games and remain undefeated through two nights of competition.

Someone told me I missed eight shots all night. She was my next opponent. I don't know if she was being literal or hitting on me to distract my game.

Just like when I go into character,"experienced vocalist and musician,"when learning to play and sing, I've used the same approach for building a deck, swinging a golf club, and now I have a new role as a player who rarely misses a shot in pool. Truthfully, I play new roles every day.

When I do any activity, I expect to watch it happen like I visualized it. The golf ball will land near the target, and the ball sinks into the right pocket as the cue ball comes to rest for the next shot.

Need

I wrote this book, knowing that my success will reflect your satisfaction from achieving meaningful change. The most visible changes happen when you have transformed your body and mind into happier and healthier versions.

I don't see how a fitness program could be any easier. I mean that in the most literal way. It couldn't be more relaxed and produce results like this. [#][#]

I have some extraordinary experiments to share. The participants gained significant muscle mass by visualizing, and Others lost weight from awareness.

Changing old beliefs is challenging, yet thought is behind everything we do. Take control and change what you believe by visualizing and vocalizing.

Diversity

There are three distinct kinds of health that you need to manage for wellness. Mental health issues are only being recognized in recent years.

It wasn't until the 1980s before we started hearing more about depression as an imbalance in the brain. This launched Prozac and anti-depressant medications that correct the problem. [#]

Neurotransmitters pass between your brain cells. In some individuals, the amount that passes through is inhibited. This causes inexplicable and enduring sadness. [#]

Hormones and Neurotransmitters

Neurotransmitters and hormones are not necessary except for how they shape everyday life and your internal operations. If you consider that kind of thing worthwhile, then I guess they're useful for remaining alive.

Look at the figure: Neurotransmitters are little messengers. The Central Nervous System uses this chemical to transmit nerve impulse across synapses like shown in the illustration: [#]

Neurotransmitters are released across the synaptic cleft, where they are received by specific receptors on the membrane of the post synaptic neuron.

Hormones factor in your behavior and attitude. They also serve the endocrine system as messengers to communicate with target cells. There is more than one kind of hormone.

Most of us have heard of Endorphins. It's the hormone that acts as an analgesic that's produced naturally as a reaction to pain. Dopamine and Oxytocin are similar chemicals created by our body to stimulate euphoric sensations.

I am investigating how my family and I can be healthy and happy for the rest of our lives. Much of what I learn has come from extensive conversations with an MD who specializes in hormone restoration. We've been under his treatment for many years.

I recommend that you seek someone like him. Doesn't the higher logic suggest that we should be aware of things that affect our mood and wellness?

Boys Don't Cry

I talk to a therapist every week. Sometimes, I need to talk over specific situations in a discussion aimed toward an end.

Other times, I need to process emotion. I admit it. I cry easily for a man. It's almost embarrassing, but I refuse to expend all my resources to keep it hidden.

It's the man who has enough confidence and wit who cries without remorse. Resistance is such a deeply rooted habit in men that it slips by awareness, and we miss the most cathartic way to expel negative energy.

Listen

Want someone to listen to you? Try paying them. If you're going to pay them, you know they'll be listening. They prepare advice based on your needs once they know them.

A therapist offers objective feedback. They reply to your concerns with remedies, a fresh perspective, or advice you hadn't duly considered.

Chapter Four: No Pain, No Gain is Caveman Logic

If you own this book, you want to help yourself, and I want to help you do that. I have the approach to get the results.

I had to get creative to find an effective way to gain without pain when my pain was on a different scale. If you don't feel some measure of "burn" from an accumulation of lactic acid, then you are not doing enough.

Weight-Loss Surgery

I'm happy for the people who get a fresh start to life and do something with it. With more people having surgery for rapid weight loss, countless lives have been saved, not only literally, but their quality of life. You have no life if you're a shut-in.

It must be like restoring the body back to factory settings. It seems like a happy ending, but it's not. It's a fresh start. This isn't the end of the journey; it's where it begins. You'll want to start by managing the side-effects of surgery, like sagging skin.

Think of your skin like clothing that was made to fit your body at its largest. Anytime you lose significant weight, you buy new clothes to fit. This book is your currency for buying a new birthday suit. Excess skin is unsightly, but now you have a higher physical capacity to do something about it.

I can't claim any foresight of this philosophy to minimize excess skin, but that makes it no less significant. The real difference is in my activity-based approach.

For as far as my skin was stretched, working all the muscles in my body every day helped to restore elasticity and muscle tone to shrink the excess skin. When you consider how much weight loss, my age, and my disability, it's an extraordinary approach to wellness because it works.

If you recall, we can condition our minds to believe anything, real or imagined. Therefore pretend resistance produces tangible results.

Imagination

It's the approach that's so effective, yet still easy enough for me. I found my way with help from a lifelong companion, my imagination.

I don't use terms like "exercise" or "workout" because they've always conjured negative images in my mind. I use more precise phrases like "conditioning" and "training."

One way to look at the difference is that conditioning is a permanent state. We can choose when to train, but we are always in a state of conditioning. It's either negative or positive, and the one you favor determines your level of wellness.

Lifting heavy weights is no longer an option. When this approach is executed correctly, imagination is no less effective than reality. Early on, I used my cane, vying muscle against muscle. That home hospital bed is still less than ten feet away from where I sit.

Enhance real activity with imagination. Imaginary resistance, ghost opponents, and phantom coaches are all part of the fictional circumstances you can use.

My internal coach is a composite of the people in my life that had a positive influence. I hear a familiar voice in my head, instructing me through the practice of a new skill. The ability to put my imagination into practical use will not go unrealized.

Throughout the development of this philosophy, I repeated many of the same activities. I don't know of one single time when I did it the same specific way.

Diet or Exercise?

To start, is it easier to focus on increasing activity, or would cutting calories be the way to go? Both are the obvious answer, but this isn't a trick.

Losing weight by cutting calories isn't the best method for me. Working against resistance, real or imagined, is irrelevant to the results it produces.

Activity produces results quicker than a diet alone. Results inspire you to eat better because it links directly to the continuation of your rapid progress.

My diet is over-simplified, but that is not by accident. If I want good health, I should eat for nutrition, but also what I like.

Don't spend a fortune to watch groceries slowly decimate in the refrigerator. You need more protein and a better variety in your diet to maintain balance. Fitness is central to all areas of life, each having its own influence on quality.

My article compared my approach to a conventional one. As I mentioned, I lost over a hundred and twenty-some pounds in less than eight months against enormous obstacles.

I started doing little things throughout the day using imaginary resistance. I pushed and pulled using muscle against muscle, or compelled movement against gravity.

That's not where it ends. For specific times allocated to health, I began doing what came to be known as *conditioning sequences.*

This tandem of practices has an aggregate effect that accelerates progress. A Philosophy that works for me will work for anyone. If you have physical limitations, then you also need something easy but effective. I don't know of anything until now that will serve you better.

Information Age

If something to accommodate my wellness needs already existed, I would know about it. I would have my copy within a minute of logging onto a computer.

The countless ways you can own books on-demand is life in the information age. Our ability to share intelligence is unprecedented.

At this moment, I am waiting for services to be restored by my internet provider. It affects almost everything. It's a reminder of how much dependence we have on the internet. It's a challenge, but more challenging times will come and go.

You won't discover data with full application to living well by coincidence. When you find it, it's a smaller part of a bigger reason.

Conventional

This isn't an instruction manual that delineates every day of the week for two months. If that's what you require, I'm sure you will find something, but not here.

There are many programs available that walk you each step of a diet and exercise plan. These do work if you follow the instructions strictly for the quantified period. No one knows better; it's unpleasant to live with restrictions.

It isn't technology keeping us overweight if these plans work. I've had to overcome those things which do, and the first thing is to identify them.

The response to my blog changed my life's course. I wanted to write fiction and may think I had a choice, but leaving this unfinished would've meant the kind of regret with which I choose not to live.

If you are looking for something that takes "thinking" out of your hands, this book isn't for you. The words only get more challenging.

Right Mind

I crudely tell myself to get my mind right. It's how I capture focus, even when it's slippery and easy to lose.

Starting with breathing, one way I begin is to employ a technique I call "*Robot-Arms.*" It's a strict, controlled motion that does not deviate in any way.

Think of a robotic arm on an assembly line. It never changes its movement, range, or speed. You'll be surprised how adding tension will cause lactic acid to produce a quick burn.

I visualize running full speed. I act it out in slow motion and use muscle-tension to stimulate my upper body. There are no limits to what you can do, except those you impose.

I've spent a lifetime developing my creativity. The trauma from my childhood was a driving factor that led to expanding my mind. Imagination is at the heart of this philosophy, and vice-versa.

Results are results, so finding a virtually effortless approach makes a practical, even preferred, choice.

Conditioning Sequences

As you recall, this is the term that replaced conventional words like "workout." Traditional language left dreadful images in my head, which worked ridiculously hard to compel a reason for me not to be active.

I never responded to an enthusiastic training partner. He shouts, "One more?" and the last one barely made it up. I couldn't catch my breath to speak, which is good because we can remain friends.

The payoff for one more is not worth it to me. C.S. are moments allocated for training at the gym, at home, with or without real resistance, and endless other ways you can be active.

How you feel and believe can trump a universal truth. The best thing you can do is not to overeat or wear tight-fitting clothes.

Going Internal

You've heard people talk about making a mind and body connection. I call it going *internal*, and it's very literal.

I visualize what is happening in the muscles being used during a sequence. I imagine blood cells scurrying around as a result of the proportionate tension I hold throughout the motion. [**]

See the above figure. Maybe it's someone you recognize from eighth-grade Biology. He's the skinless man from the textbook.

Have you ever looked over the muscles in the human body? You don't have to know when you're working deltoids or pectoral muscles. Keep it simple, shoulders and chest mean the same thing. You will learn by default, so no worries.

Ideally, work every area of the body every day. It's never an all-out effort. Laborers develop lean muscular bodies by default of their profession.

Learning is positive conditioning for your brain. It gets stimulation from understanding and knowledge. Of all muscles, it's your heart and brain that needs conditioning the most.

Specialized Training

We all have different motives, and an effective routine is commensurate with your feelings about it. Remember dread? It will come knocking if it catches a whiff of discomfort.

This approach is the most relaxed ever introduced to produce real results so quickly in my experience.

It Counts, Whether You Do or Not

A man approached me with questions at the gym. I explained the philosophy and its nature. His expression livened when I told him that I never count anything, including sets, reps, minutes, or miles. He declared it liberating.

I commented that showing me how many calories I burned wasn't an incentive for me. It was the opposite. I was discouraged from learning I worked that hard and hadn't burnt off 16 ounces of soda.

That number is depressing and insignificant. We are changing our thermostat setting to naturally burn more calories at rest and all the time, not while we are laboring on a treadmill.

How does that Make You Feel?

Tight clothes make you feel fat. Put on something loose and nonrestrictive. Try never to overeat. Our universe feels and responds to feelings. Feeling lean hastens progress while feeling fat or bloated impedes it.

I considered accepting a new body image because hearing words like "workout" caused my back to hurt and dread to take hold.

I have a beautiful wife, and we have three beautiful kids together. For all intents and purposes, I'm off the market. I even joked it was my duty to gain weight. I never was that funny.

How many others are there like me, or worse? They're in pain from their back and extra weight. Their self-esteem often takes a beating. Comments from influential family members are the knockout blows that keep hope abated.

Better than Nothing

Doing something is better than nothing. This is where I started before evolving into the philosophy that is now a book. I kept it simple and easy.

Acclimating to change is best done slowly. "Just do something," became my mantra. This is how I discovered the power of using words to reinforce and create a new belief to facilitate changes in existing views.

The way I was approaching fitness was vastly different because I have no specific sequence or predetermined plan. I never worry about making progress. I assume I am. I feel it in my throbbing muscles and my swollen veins. There's a burn, but it's far from painful.

A conditioning sequence centers on the best ways to stimulate adaptation safely. Intuitive training is how the best of the best will train. Those who are self-aware represent the athlete of the future.

The Little Things

Much of my activity happens in brief moments as permitted. I may be at my desk, stepping on an elastic band and doing curls, or driving down the highway and using a resistance band attached to the passenger seat. You will be amazed at how quickly it adds up.

Let the approach affect how you feel about being healthy. Who would argue that healthy people are not the sexiest people?

Guaranteed Success

If you follow through, you will see results. Success is guaranteed in your commitment. You're the guarantee for us both.

I have failed many people if I fall short of spreading information that produces positive results so quickly and so easily.

I've heard many say they believe I'm onto something special. When you see the dramatic physical changes I've made, remember they're small compared to the less visible changes.

If I can turn it around from a long recovery and a sedentary lifestyle forced upon me by a bad back, then anyone can. Like everything, it starts in our minds. I had to change how my mind was working. I had to do some rewiring.

Change Nothing, Nothing Changes

Let me ask, where do you expect to be in twelve months? Looking back to last year at this time may help you answer. Unless you want to repeat the same answer next year, something needs to change.

When you change nothing, nothing changes. If you commit yourself to change and do something, you have a guarantee commensurate with that commitment. If you dedicate yourself, you succeed. You can completely transform yourself in under a year.

Muscle-tone

I found a study online from an experiment conducted by an Ivy League school that's exciting, especially for the physically impaired. It was a model experiment, where two groups are selected, the control group and the experimental group. Both are groups that have a simple goal: increase muscle percentage.

The Control group was led by a certified fitness trainer and had access to a full gym. Routines were mapped out, and they were required to spend at least an hour in the gym, five days a week.

The Experimental group was taken to a practitioner who specialized in meditative exercises. He gathered subjects in a room lit by candlelight. They were told to relax in the comfortable seating.

The sound of Tibetan bowls played in the background as the instructor walked them through meditation and then onto the visualization process. He helped them paint mental images after he had guided them into a state-of-mind that is optimal for results.

Their guide gave them a complete tour of their body's muscular system. He used words that promote positive thinking and enable belief. The guide added details in their visualizations the first time and gave them advice about incorporating sensory input.

Success is when the mind believes that the body is at work, triggering adaptation, or the creation of more muscle.

When the trial ended, the control group added an average of 30% muscle. The experimental group added an average of 15% muscle. It's half as much, but if it takes twice as long, is that really a problem?

You Should Be Dancing

You know the experience;you insert headphones, hit play on your wireless media, and hear a drumbeat. As it grows louder, it feels in sync with your heart. Other instruments join in concert for a surround sound experience.

Music is a recognized form of energy. I'm not sure how it's categorized, does it matter? A melody can generate body impulse reactions. Anyone who likes to dance will agree that music compels movement.

Move to the beat and let the rhythm set your pace. In no time, you will transition seamlessly from one motion to another.

Cadence

Cadence is the rhythmic flow in sequence;it's a conditioning sequence. Use music to set your pace and guide your motions.

You can use your playlist to keep you on schedule. Another good use of a music playlist is when you position songs in a strategic order, plan for a faster cadence in the high point of your training arc.

An arc is the three stages of a conditioning sequence: warm-up, work, and cool down. Don't put yourself in a position where you need to rush. I would rather be late than show up on time but frazzled. It's essential to plan for a few extra minutes to transition into and out of your optimal state-of-mind.

Mind Over Matters

University researchers sought to prove weight-loss is mind over matter using two independent housekeeping staffs from hotels in neighboring cities. These women were moderately overweight and the ideal subjects for this experiment.

At orientation, they were given a device to wear throughout the trial. The instructions were simple. They were told to maintain the same routine and lifestyle.

They were in the dark about the device they had to wear every day, and plug in twice a week to transmit data.

Experimental Group

Both groups went home under the same premise. However, researchers summoned the experimental group back, where they are given insight into what the device measures and given full disclosure of what the device measures and how it works.

Researchers imbued them with a little fiction to enhance the placebo effect. They told them that the supplements they were testing had a fat-burning combination. They were given caffeine tablets to produce a stimulating effect.

When they explained the purpose of the experiment, they made it seem centered around the placebo drug. They were each given a written guarantee of weight loss. It's meaningless unless the participants think otherwise. Then, it powers up their confidence.

They didn't need to know that, and all questions were redirected with reinforcing statements. They were told to start thinking like a lean person.

The women in the experiment believed they didn't get enough exercise and had a poor diet. When the test was complete, the difference in the results of the two groups was phenomenal.

Both groups followed virtually the same schedule. The control group does not receive anything new; therefore, no change in belief, no change in behavior, no changes.

They were each weighed before participation began and had a minimal variance at their starting weight.

When the trial had run its course, the experimental group lost over seventy pounds. The control group gained two pounds collectively. Any difference in physical demands would be negligible, meaning awareness was the key to their weight loss.

Maid a Difference

Researchers educated one group and left the other in the dark. One group received vital data and used it. They adapted how they felt about working. Feeling lean, thinking like a thin person is how it all starts.

Tale of Two Hotels

How many people approach housework and think of it as a fitness routine? I didn't always, but the results from this testing are reliable enough logic for that to change.

No longer will I wield a broom or mop for only one reason: to make dirty floors clean.

As I heal, I plan to do all manner of house and yard work in a way that increases my heart rate or builds muscle-tone. I pretend things are more challenging than they are and exaggerate my motion.

The right perception is a catalyst for change. Stop seeing house and yard work as dreaded chores. Housekeeping is the most thankless job on the planet. We only notice when it's not done. That missing gratitude becomes less important because of what else you accomplish.

Mind Matters

Any action requiring skill activates brain cells called neurons. Neurons fire in a specific sequence along a particular pathway. When you find the correct path to successfully execute the best motion for the task, stop over thinking. If you have done it, you can do it, so have faith your body knows exactly what to do, and proceed without delay.

When your mind has too many things to consider, it's overloaded. Brain cells misfire. When we over think what we're doing, doubt is present. Confidence has a natural ebb and flow. When absent, your performance suffers.

Practical Activity

You can condition yourself positively by doing housework at high speed. If you move from here to there in less time, you're building endurance. It's a small step, but it's in the right direction.

Using light or imaginary resistance with a broom-handle would be a positive form of conditioning. If you can accomplish tasks while exaggerating your movements or moving in slow motion while holding tension, it's just as effective, only you would have a cleaner floor.

Keep steady pressure throughout a full range of motion to benefit. While there is no wrong way to be active, there is a good, better, and best way.

Third-person Critique

Try stepping outside yourself to evaluate your behaviors as if they belonged to someone else. You must embrace the truth. You need to be 100% honest with yourself. Even legitimate reasons are excuses. I live with constant pain from using poor judgment when I was younger.

Complaining only returns negative energy, and it made me unpleasant to be around.

When you can own behaviors that caused the consequences you suffer, you will liberate your spirit from guilt. The energy we exhaust searching for blame, when we already know, is time wasted for nothing.

When we look back on a moment, we usually learn how we could've done something differently, which would've changed the outcome to one preferred. See Scripting.

Powerful emotions steal reason from your mind's internal dialogue, making it easy to exacerbate circumstances by forgetting discretion in favor of candor.

Priceless Gift

Emotion, especially emotion that has set in, like depression, can distort perception. Life is a gift, the biggest treasure we can own. I live better than most.

Not because I have vast wealth. Not because of where I was born or to whom. I live a good life for a good reason. I'm sharing that reason now.

I've learned the skills to see life differently. I discovered that we shine brighter as a result of the darkness. I know the method involved in making positive changes permanent.

That's priceless when the skills are transferrable; it's a procedure. If you qualify as a human, you can learn it and reap the advantages.

Chapter Five: A Lifetime of Relationships

The most important relationship is the one you have with your higher power and yourself. Your mother is the most critical person when you first enter the world. A father becomes a more significant influence over time and peaks after puberty.

Your higher power will vary as any reader. Some of you believe in God; others choose atheism or Darwinism, and the agnostics are those who do not feel strongly in either way. This is the fastest-growing population in Western civilization.

It's your business, but you should have some belief beyond what you can see. You can't see the wind, but you can see its effects. Just call it your higher self if you struggle with it.

Self-esteem is the measure of how you feel about you. It's easy to get caught up in self-pity. We need to defend against it, and you need self-love for that. You must love yourself before you can love another, but don't become full of yourself.

Can you be honest with yourself? Not everyone can or is. Don't embellish to make the truth to be more or less. Don't exaggerate facts to reflect achievement when nothing was achieved.

If you don't get real now, you'll fail. You haven't done anything so wrong in your life that it's unforgivable. You can adopt an experience that makes everything in life more comfortable, even sleep.

It has been my experience with this philosophy that misfortune is easier to accept, and incidentals are simpler to manage. Sometimes, it's like circumstances conspired to aid in my personal development. I have demonstrated proven results for you to witness over a timeline that goes back years.

Childhood

Your brain acquires information in life's early stages. It comes in many way sand from many sources. Unfiltered data is absorbed directly into your sub-conscious.

Childhood is life's most formative years. The most influential person in our lives is our mother. These years are critical to the development of our personality.

Proper nurturing direct you toward becoming an adult. Free will is a variable, and choices and chance to intervene as a smaller part of a bigger reason. The future is what you choose it to be today.

I was injured by emotional trauma in my early years, but fault has no part in it. The consequences are all mine. The quality of my future will be determined by those consequences.

Blank Slate

Today is the anniversary of the day I was born. It's a common belief that you come out with a blank slate. I think it's logical enough to consider. What would you see on your slate?

What has been added, and how much would you like to erase? Most importantly, what are you planning to add now?

Most people know that forgiveness is something you do for you more than it is for them. You must include forgiving yourself, which is not easy for everyone.

Emotional Landfill

I was exposed to a lot of explosive hostility during my childhood. While my needs were met and my parents loved me, I was collateral damage in their conflicts.

My mother never loved my father. I picked up on it with what she would say, like, "I don't love your father."

I was too young to interact in adult matters. My father isn't innocent, but what I've heard my mother say still makes me shudder.

Mothers never intend harm, but intention doesn't moderate the injury. I was unable to comprehend the drama attached to episodic depression.

Emotion consumed her and robbed her of sound judgment. She forgot that I was only a boy and didn't have the mental faculty for what she needed.

I wanted to show her love, but I didn't like being near her when she was depressed. She would grow frustrated with me for not wanting to be involved in an alliance against Dad. It made me angry at her. In my mind, he was the stable parent.

I was a prisoner in a broken home. I would stay in my room for hours. I would hear them fighting and pray that they would get divorced.

I heard a story about something my father did before I was born. I never expected he was always a good man. He ended those behaviors and found joy in buying, selling, and trading. He quit drinking, stopped smoking, and sometimes, he would go to bed before sunset.

I've always felt my father earned forgiveness for whatever he did. My father may have been immature and foolish at one time, and he has struggled with the truth, but my mother was the monster to me.

My Dad passed away without warning in 1999, just months short of turning Sixty. We may have never shared a meaningful conversation, but I loved him, and he'll always be missed.

To Whom do You Look?

The nature of your relationships changes significantly over a lifetime. When you're young, you're learning. You need to know certain things, and you look to your parents or guardian for answers. At this stage, we need to find our identity. If we don't declare, one will be assigned. Unwanted labels are rarely unearned. Young people turn to friends for the answers they didn't get at home.

These friends often have similar issues, and the best way to connect is self-medicating under the guise of partying. It can become a dangerous routine suddenly.

Co dependence

Some mothers have so much love for their babies that they go too far. I call it "Big-heart syndrome" because it's misguided love. Mom discovers how her behavior stunted her child's development only after it has been done.

She instinctively wants to shield them from the world, but it's a world they need to know. This is a general condition not exclusive to mothers. It's called *co dependence*.

I was quiet while my wife made sacrifices that seemed extreme. She felt strongly about what she was doing. It would've aroused her anger toward me if I questioned her judgment as a parent. I avoid confrontation when I can, but that wasn't the time for me to be silent.

From a rear-view mirror, it's clear how she had a destructive influence that inhibited child development. While we are all ultimately responsible for ourselves, it's harder when imperfect people strive too hard for a perfect life.

Mothers, resist your instinct to intervene. Allow your child to live with fewer limitations. Sparing them from a painful moment now could be divesting them of experience they come to need later.

Fathers, do not be afraid of rocking the boat. This is a problem much bigger than a risk of capsizing. As parents, we are obliged to guide our offspring through all stages, from infancy to healthy adults. We work with what we know.

My wife and I are fortunate to have children who gave us no trouble through those tough years of adolescence. Our family is connected by bonds that are interwoven within the family unit. I don't see my family scattered across the country. I think we will always be close.

Synonym for Failure

Children must be free to fail. It's how they learn and will shape into life experience. Most mothers are needed less with age. She needs to be reminded that she matters. Most mothers will do the best they can with what they know.

In our home, love is abundant. It smooths over the rough patches as they arise. You weren't put on this earth to spend it alone. We're capable of love; we can express it, feel it, and communicate it through language. Procreation is instinctive for species survival and pair-bonding.

In order of importance, relationships are not so far behind your health. A few close relationships have a significant impact on life-quality. A long, healthy, life alone would be no life.

Long-Term Commitments

My wife and I have been together for about three decades. The honeymoon is over. Complacency is the biggest risk. However, even after all this time, our relationship is quite the contrary.

We have drawn closer, discovering each other on deeper levels, especially in recent years. There is no absolute right or wrong way. There are only the choices you make and the consequences. Choose happiness and love. It bears a brighter tomorrow.

Couples aren't meant to agree on everything. We learn more about each other in conflict than during peace. Disagreements, the need to be right, and ineffective communications are bundled into the legalese, *irreconcilable differences*. It has taken over as the top reason for divorce among Americans.

Our children have grown into adults. The exit strategy from the nest has already begun. They don't need us as much or in the same way anymore.

My wife and I will share our lives and need to rediscover our relationship. At this stage, our vision of the future should align. Love is more natural when you are headed in the same direction. When love is real, real love is enough.

If you want the most from sharing your life with another person, get on the same page. When your partner's actions make you suspicious, don't always assume guilt.

See the situation for itself, understand it, then choose an appropriate response. Patience is a lost treasure. Do you have the will to pull back your emotions? Can you assess a situation objectively? You may be upset now, so install a trigger to remember your love in these moments.

If you can't find common ground or reach an impasse, it's okay to revisit the subject later. It might not be wise to let it simmer overnight. Giving yourself a couple of hours to lose emotion should be enough. In love, when both try, a happier bond is guaranteed.

It's helpful to have common interests, but it doesn't determine the success of a relationship. Even the length of a relationship is not a real measure of success. A successful pair-bond is when you grow up, grow old, and grow together. The support comes from both directions.

When you understand your companion's intent, it's easier to accept flaws as just part of it. Disagreements happen when more than one mind is involved. It's not an unhealthy thing as people may think.

Hostilities

Hostility is always a threat to injure someone whom you love. Never attack someone's character. If you feel exasperated and raise your voice, do you expect a tight embrace, or do you think return fire is more likely? Is that what you want? Neither do our partners. Your goal should center on resolution.

To what end does hostility lead? What we think is urgent is trivial. It's a high price to pay for nothing, exacting its toll on you in hindsight. Keep in mind that words are often intended differently than they're interpreted. Any dispute that escalates results from neither of you remembering love. It takes an instant to go from 0 to angry at times.

When people draw instant conclusions based on a shred of evidence and assume how their partner will react, they'll become angry over speculation. This kind of dispute can be minimized but no winning. It's like watching your opponent run the table and win the game before you take your first shot.

Secret Secrets

We all have secrets. How much we share is an unpredictable variant without a look behind the curtain. Never accept life at face value. When we keep secrets from our mate, it is like leaving negative energy in the dark. Darkness, or silence, creates optimal conditions for rapid growth.

Plan a day of amnesty, and set guidelines, and open up to the bare-bones truth. Many of the reasons we become hostile have nothing to do with our mate. Communicating sensitive issues is a skill that successful relationships will master.

You must avoid letting your past compromise your future if it creates suspicion that has a destructive influence. Trust is vital, and when it is breached, it damages you and your mate. Love, truth, patience, understanding, and awareness are all qualities you should share with your lover.

If you are exclusive or married, then all your sexual fantasies are now a matter between you and one other person for life. Break from routine and develop a willingness for new experiences. It takes effort, and you do not need to push the envelope every time.

However, if you do not know your boundaries, how will you know when you have broken them? It's a thin line separating too much from too little. Use it or lose it is another universal truth.

The Line

Take the time to talk about the line, where it is, and what it means; define it for each other. If you and this person plan to spend your lives together, establish clear boundaries from the beginning.

Learn how to manage tense moments when you disagree or have a grievance. Agreeing to disagree is possible unless someone needs to be right. A right-fighter will abandon rationality to defend their position.

Agreeing to specific terms during conflict starts with acknowledging that love is why this person is in your life. You can work out what is and is not okay.

We want the same security we give. There are no ultimatums unless the intention is real. Going there too often is unhealthy in every way.

Unless you intend to part from this person, then be silent about it. No one does it for the sake of the other's happiness, which is often suggested.

Same Old Dance

Can we learn a new way to communicate, or are we forever prisoners to the same dance? At this point in a relationship, you have moved past infidelity issues and enabled trust. That is vital. Without it, a couple cannot move forward.

Show a willingness to own behaviors; replace being right with an effort to seek resolution. Making this a practice will go a long way to increase the peace.

Rules of Engagement

You will find it useful to establish a few rules you both agree before committing to lifetime exclusivity. Make disagreements about what you learn in finding a resolution. You will become adept at de-escalating and defusing the powder keg that could result in a very harmful interaction.

There are many reasons couples fight, money, sex, jealousy, and more throughout the relationship. Learn boundaries to do it healthfully. The other option is to be another statistic for failed relationships.

React or Respond?

When we are threatened, we can react or respond. These words have different connotations. If a doctor tells you that you reacted to a drug, it isn't good news. However, if you responded to treatment, it means it is useful.

Communicating with the right words means knowing connotations and can make the difference between practical expression and misinterpretation. Listening happens far too rare in an egocentric culture. The words we use, how we use them, and to whom, become the measure of your social intelligence.

There are many forms of intelligence, and we can improve upon them all, contingent on circumstance. Most of our limits are set by only one provider – our minds.

Awareness of the self incites genuine confidence in your abilities. You are not afraid to be wrong when you are comfortable with your intellect.

These moments decrease in frequency and end when you can concede to a new belief because a better logic exists. Correct your thinking when better thinking exists.

NOT Time to Bundle

If hard feelings are discovered in some other area, it's not time to bundle it into the moment as if it were relevant. Don't drag the past out into the light.

Ideally, we should be on the same team, remember this type of disagreement, and plan an exit strategy. It'll mean nothing tomorrow unless it escalates. Irrelevant issues confuse the real problem. It's a defense tactic called redirecting.

There is never a good time to remind your partner of his or her flaws. You can be reasonably sure they're already familiar from the previous times you listed them, to have been there when they happened.

If these are things you have moved past, what are you doing back here? To make it a point to list them again is intentionally counter-productive.

This is a time allocated to settle one specific grievance. You can't do that if you are resuming old behaviors. Don't keep these memories alive. They should be resting in peace, never to be vocalized for any reason that disparages the forgiven.

Save other topics for moments when you are feeling well. The ideal time to discuss sensitive matters is different for different couples. Go into it with an open mind and a willingness to forgive and to apologize. In a serious relationship, reaffirm your dedication. You cannot build a system for managing tempers when one of you keeps losing it.

Emotion Trumps Rationality

This is a version of you wearing thick glasses in dense clouds, and your vision is impaired by the moment, making you a liability for saying something you'll regret. Anger will come and go, but love is forever.

If one of us has apologized and the other has forgiven, then the infraction evaporates and is no longer available for use.

Argumente de Futile

Everyone should learn the skills to improve communication. Uniting in mind and purpose is a great place to start. What used to be good enough in a relationship does not remain that way. As time passes, we want and deserve more.

Acquire sufficient composure to overcome emotion. Recognize the situation for that which it is really. This is one reason why a couple should be relatively close on an intellectual level. In its absence, a new dynamic involving manipulation will become a theme in the relationship.

Change is Simply Constant

For as difficult as it is, transformation is a simple process. It is the continued routine of positive reinforcement for the acquisition of your desired behavior.

This leads you to achieve. Improvement means learning how to temper negative thoughts and actions, especially when they are self-destructive. Continuous learning and heightened awareness will keep you inspired and motivated.

Practice the good, dismiss the bad. It's simple after you gain competence in transitioning your state of mind into optimal for performing the necessary skill.

If it seems too comfortable, it should. Don't start second-guessing whether it is working. It is. It gets easier as your physical, mental, and emotional conditions improve.

Plan

Do everything possible to improve your relationships. I get positive feedback from every direction, especially from those who fill my life. Few things are more precious than family.

I'm confident in my intellect and can admit when I'm wrong. There's no shame. It happens only when you are human. If I believe I'm right, it's challenging to resist defending my position, despite knowing better.

I should let it go or agree to disagree. Kindness and compromise are not weaknesses. They are intelligence incarnate. Compromise is a simple concept: if we take, we must give. We must be kind before expecting kindness.

An invaluable tool in my research is a book that has two religions based on it. The Bible cannot be discarded for its divine wisdom. It teaches improved awareness, along with a comprehensive understanding of the human condition.

This heightened awareness helps to foster changes within the family unit and develop a new harmony in how we interact and cohabitate. I have no affiliation with organized religion, but I have studied this phenomenal achievement in depth.

Burden of Beauty

It's easy for a man to get caught up in lustful thoughts at the sight of an attractive woman. I am not discounting same-sex attraction, just keeping it simple.

A beautiful woman who posts suggestive pictures will get attention from men. Sadly, this behavior is symptomatic of a girl who grew up without the care and positive influence of a male role model.

The number of crude comments alone is too high to read them all. While she's feeling adored, she's objectified. It's a trade she's willing to make.

After a certain age, a pattern of thought develops and affects her belief system. As the number of comments and likes begins to decline, she internalizes it as having already peaked.

It's difficult for a woman who has used her beauty to make her way through life to accept the effects of aging gracefully.

Every new birthday begins another cycle of anxiety. Her worry intensifies with each year. Her vision of the future is living alone, and one cat shy of a baker's dozen.

Thirty-Year-Old Women

Women who contact me through social media with romantic inclinations have an average age of Thirty. It's a landmark age and a turning-point in a woman's life. There isn't enough blush to hide her fading youth.

Once her twenties are behind her, perspectives change. Around then, the expiration on child-bearing years has entered view. It generally leads to over thinking everything because she is overwhelmed. Panic distorts perception.

Her vision of all that still needs to happen is endless only in a smaller window of time. Feelings of being pitted against time stimulate severe anxiety. She needs to change her thinking to avoid one of her greatest fears: settling for less.

Desperation is one sure way to impair your judgment, especially if you are seeking a permanent companion. That isn't a decision you want to rush. You'd live much better with stability, security, and disposable income.

Unfortunately, there's no big selection left, and there are legitimate, possibly unsavory, reasons a man is into his thirties or forties, but has never been married.

At forty, you're fertile, but the quality of your eggs drops off sharply. The chance of congenital disabilities or miscarriage is higher the longer you wait.

The women I've met are pretty enough to attract handsome men. These men are charming, smooth, and say just the right things. A woman can be enchanted by a man's demeanor. It's easy to forget that a handsome man is just as attractive to other women.

These women are masterful seductresses and have the brains and beauty to lure your man into a situation where he doesn't belong. Men are weak-willed when sexual gratification is available.

She keeps her heart closely guarded because she has given it before to have it returned to her in pieces. Trust issues will make it difficult for her to have a real relationship that lasts until she learns to trust again. When a heart has been betrayed, it leaves a bitter taste.

She has an excellent reason not to trust, but justification is not much of a consolation for the loss of real intimacy shared with your lover, not just another partner.

Most of these women tell me they're seeking a man with my profile because they want someone trustworthy. She wants to acquire stability that few men around her age can offer.

These highly desirable ladies looking for real love, knowing they may not be perceived the same way if a man knows too much about her truth, will have many secrets.

It's a lifestyle from which it's hard to break free. Men will be reluctant to commit to the kind of woman who openly talks about their sexual desires online. They only like it in the moment, not for anything serious. Ladies, this is the gospel truth.

Men will not choose you. Like me, I preferred a girl with much less experience. You can't change your past, but it's a matter of proper discretion. You can choose to share or not. History shouldn't destine the future.

Some women are compelled into exotic dancing and doing things for men; it's not about sex, it's a need for money that goes for gas, groceries, tuition, and providing for someone who depends on her.

Trust?

How does anyone find an honest man (person) today? It gets tricky. How do you know? Good, honest men and distasteful men behave much the same way when you meet. How will you know who is genuine and who is genuinely a good actor?

You always withdraw before involving your heart. You stop it when you catch yourself thinking about him being handsome, kind, and congenial. It seems hard to imagine this kind soul could hurt you.

Then you are reminded of who else had those qualities when you met. Something in you will not allow you to trust. The hurt from last time still lingers. Don't allow your new man to become your former in your eyes. You are choosing to live with constant suspicion and anxiety.

Stop before you start checking his jacket and pants pockets, his wallet, and even his phone. You justify your invasion of his privacy due to your past experiences, not his. Suspicion kills relationships.

Family Unit

A companion who believes in me will own my world. I have one. I know a husband's role well. I am a father who improved upon the part since becoming one.

As you know, from conception beyond the toddler years, the mother is the primary caregiver. The father is secondary only to her, but he plays a vital role the mother cannot.

Dad's role increases in the lives of his children at a rate commensurate with age and maturity. That applies to the kids as well.

Daughters who have the influence of a positive male role model will have more confidence. She gains authentic self-respect and learns patience for her kids and her mate. She is more independent and will never allow herself to be mistreated.

A boy who has a positive male role model will learn how to treat women and learn his gender role in society by emulating the proper behavior.

I try to do the right thing. As cliché as it sounds, it gets easier. I am always striving to be the best version of myself.

I know who I am. I'm a loving person, a faithful husband, an affectionate father, and I'm a free spirit. I'm creative, I'm an author, an actor, and I'm living with purpose. All of this is summed up to say, I'm happy. You should know who you are and who you want to be.

I'm continuing toward the next best version of myself. With each improvement, I can upgrade my status. I'm not a perfectionist and don't expect to see it in this world.

Every day I want to be a positive influence in my life and the lives of those around me. A life of love, family, and good friends is a treasure. However, it may be fun to gather with friends, compared to family, it's a beer commercial. We can choose our friends. We have no choice with family, but ideally, a natural bond will form from love.

From birth, we depend on someone for our needs. That job hopefully falls to a pair of people from whom you received your DNA.

All new parents share a few behaviors. Most tend to go overboard for the first and last born. The firstborn gets a lot of attention because parents are learning their role as a parent. That tends to cause overcompensation by a parent who feels guilt, warranted or otherwise.

The last born is the baby. Parents have matured and acquired more resources. The last child is the beneficiary of all the groundwork laid by their siblings. Be alert to jealousy among middle-children. They often feel like an oversight. They crave more attention.

Raising Little Humans

There are more changes to the human anatomy in the womb and during the first twelve months than any other time. From the moment of conception, two bloodlines are united. This sperm and egg tandem hold the genetic blueprint for whom we become before external influences take effect.

I think life begins as soon as the process starts moving forward—the moment when these cells unit starts the process of living energy. A new life has begun.

You inherit genetic predispositions from the merging of two bloodlines. In most places around the world, there is no reason to question your heritage. If you were born in Russia, you are Russian.

This aspect is unique to the Western Hemisphere, particularly the United States. We could have the ancestry, of which we are unaware.

We hope for a healthy mix of positive traits from the dominant genes. A hybrid race has proven to have higher constitutions than those who descended from the same ancestry.

Child Surveillance

I had major surgery during the summer when all three kids were at home. They still needed adult supervision. Daycare was unavoidable at times, but when they were home, I needed a way to keep up with them without being physically present.

The answer was a four-camera surveillance system. I could see in every direction outside the house. More importantly, with the camera's microphone sensitivity, I could hear them even when I couldn't see them.

Disabled not Unable

I discovered a feature more useful than babysitting. I had an ear on my kids. The microphones made their interactions susceptible to being overheard wherever they went around the house.

If I heard them raise their voices in anger, I would listen. If they could not work it out, they brought the problem to me. It was never about invading their privacy.

I would hear both sides and render judgment. I had structured a successful model of the U.S. judiciary system, except I rendered decisions fairly. Sentencing was rarely necessary.

Kids will disagree when playing. They don't have the skills to negotiate and work out a compromise yet. They get angry and start talking over each other. Everyone was being heard, but no one was listening, except me.

This system gave them a place to air their frustration. Everyone could speak freely without being challenged half-way through a sentence.

There were no interruptions, and repeat offenders would be held in contempt. That could mean listening to me lecture for the next twenty-five to forty-five minutes. No one wanted that.

In these moments, you want your children to respond to you. It helps to add a bit of theatrics to give them a glimpse of how part of the world works.

The one who had the grievance became the plaintiff; his or her sibling became the defense. Each could tell their side of what happened, present any evidence or testimony by a neutral sibling.

There is no better judgment rendered than an informed one. My kids have always been honest. Although I already heard everything, I listened to both sides tell their version of the truth.

This experience taught us all something. In every dispute, there is at least one point when each participant could've done something different that would have halted escalation.

They respond to logic with a collective understanding. Logic is useful to help guide and correct behavior. It's easy to reason, "cohabitation is better for all if all make a better effort."

Until Death?

Happiness with one person can be achieved, but you're foolish to believe it happens by default. One thing I would recommend for any relationship is learning to communicate effectively and with compassion.

If you're not approachable, you will not be approached. He or she wants to feel safe talking to you about potentially sensitive matters. Save the grief and be honest about how you feel and what you want. Your mate is entitled to know if you plan on including them in your plans.

It may be awkward at first, but when you start getting to know your partner on deeper levels, happiness makes it all worthwhile.

Chapter Six: Sex

Does one vagina feel different than another to a man during intercourse? All other factors removed, if he closed his eyes, it could be anyone, and he wouldn't notice. It's an impersonal experience until we involve our minds.

How you feel about your partner makes the difference in the quality of relations. Your attraction incites greater arousal through your thinking. A quality lover is a thoughtful lover.

Let your mind participate, and your finish will be memorable. When your mind is drawn into the moment, the moment may involve one or more orgasms.

Sex has long been perceived as a physical act. It may appear valid, but without involving thought, the greatest source of pleasure is lost. Stay in the moment, or your experience will be bland.

Our inherent nature to advance the species is the same force driving us to pair-bond. Love is the most powerful energy in the universe. A love-connection between two people can be declared for life. The vows should be sacred. The words "Should be" and "is" part company here.

Frequent encounters contribute to your overall health. People who have more sex are happier. It's easy to think we place too much value on sex, but that's a myth cooked up by people who attached any sex with fornication.

"**F**ornication **U**nder **C**onsent of the **K**ing" formed an acronym originating in the dark ages. Now, it's a word, which has many contexts.

Sex is a physical expression of affection that alters one's state like a drug. Sex and intimacy are raw materials in the foundation of an enduring relationship. These are the moments we are susceptible to love.

According to the latest data, three times a week is the minimum number for life. The frequency should be higher for those short of age forty.

Many people wonder if a larger man has an advantage. Yes, he does. However, it's not in the way you might expect.

It's a matter of perception. Men made size an issue, and women tend to indulge men until it is adopted as true for both genders.

It doesn't take a large man to please a woman because the most sensitive part of a woman is within the first two inches.

If size was important, how can a finger or two bring her to orgasm? You don't need a large penis. You don't need a penis at all.

Both genders love giving and receiving oral sex, but too much of a good thing is not a good thing, especially for a woman. But then, neither is too little. Ladies, do you both a favor and speak up. Tell your man what you want. Leaving him guessing affects his confidence and a measurable decrease in pleasure. Guessing has no place in love-making.

Men, regardless of experience, depending on a woman's feedback. It doesn't have to be words that let us know we found the right place.

Don't change what works, but don't stay with one thing too long. Going to the well too often results in a dry well. Sex is subject to diminishing returns. That isn't the same as saying there are diminishing returns; everything is a matter of choice.

He may be a good lover without help. Does that mean he couldn't be tailored to your specific desires?

Touch, sight, and smell are the senses most involved in sexual congress. However, try to involve all your senses to achieve a full, sexually gratifying experience.

Finally, listen. Two ears, one mouth, blah, blah. Listen to him, listen to her. It's okay if it's not always verbal. We give away clues.

For as much as men love to make a woman whimper, scream, and every sound in between. Silence is the loudest sound because it could mean one of two things.

Look at her face. If her eyes are open and looking at you and not smiling, just wink, and change whatever you are doing now. You are not achieving the desired results.

If her eyes are closed, her chest is heaving, you can hear her breathing, and her lips are slightly parted; she is enjoying whatever you're doing, continue or quicken the pace.

My wife had never known an orgasm before we met. Now, she knows that women can not only have a powerful orgasm, but they can have more than one.

A woman can have a different kind of orgasm altogether. It releases Oxytocin, the love drug hormone that alters your mood like a real drug.

What causes love? Chemically, it's no different than eating chocolate. Every situation will be different, but it seems that it all begins from physical attraction upon which one acts and the other responds.

A pair of positive responses, and we have the seed for what could become a single entity. Let me just say there is an excellent reason why it is often called "making love." The term alone gives it away.

Make Love

I love sex. I've learned all the health benefits sex offers, but there is more. The positive effect it has had on my relationship has guided me through two decades of loyal dedication to one woman.

Sex elevates the level of affection I feel for my wife on a biological scale. She came into the marriage with minimal sexual experience. She was not aware of just how vital sexuality is as part of a couple.

Like many women, she underestimated the value sex has on the relationship. Some women don't see how love can blossom from lust. Lust is a strong sexual attraction to another person. It has taken on negative connotations because it is linked to sin or fornication.

Any relationship starts with physical attraction. Physical intimacy is an expression of affection. Abundant affection reassures that your relationship is on the right track.

The Way to a Man's Heart

The way to a man's heart doesn't come from a well-cooked meal. It's helpful, but not enough. You can only imagine my happiness to hear my wife agreeing that sex is essential to our relationship.

Circumstances can prevail that requires exceptions, but between two healthy adults, we should be together three times a week. An achievable goal.

Even the research agreed that real love is founded through physical touch in the bedroom. It may not be intercourse only, and there would be other factors.

Sex is, and will always be, the most powerful and most consistent way to win a man's love. Speaking as a man, I know it's what keeps me interested. I have such appreciation of how our species procreate. There's nothing more intimate that can happen between two people.

A woman isn't nearly as visual as a man, so they have less interest in porn. Most savvy women know not to judge a man from this behavior because both good men and bad have lustful tendencies.

It's these feelings that keep the spark burning brightly for my wife of twenty-seven years. She is making the connection between sex and the nature of our relationship in other areas.

Sex is the Foundation

When you are looking at the prospect of having the same partner to fulfill all your sexual needs, you need to make sure you are compatible and have a partner who is willing enough.

If not adequately nurtured, sex can grow stale and become much less frequent over time. For some, it has become a routine that rarely changes.

An online industry preys on these married people, explicitly encouraging them to have an affair. Many marriages today begin with agreements that declare the first year a trial.

Adult toys aren't your competition; they're your friends. If you learn how to use them, you will show her a kind of pleasure you cannot duplicate. Try as you might, you will never vibrate.

In articles merged from Men's Health and Women's Health, they report that sex is an extremely healthy activity. It's right for you in many ways. This act of procreation is born of instinct and lust, which evolves into something more significant over time. It's a foundation for real love.

They continued to report that frequent orgasms protect against Cancer. They tell us that both genders are happier when they have more sex.

It does take real skill to keep the same woman satisfied 2-3 times a week every week for life, but I've been up to the challenge.

Some women love to be humiliated in fantasy, where no rules or reputations exist. Act your fantasies out with your lover in a bolder way.

My imagination is a gift. I can live truthfully under fictional circumstances. I have many characters that can play a variety of roles. A woman wants a man who is far less considerate at times.

There's no shame that some women fantasize about being manhandled, humiliated, and forced into something that she hates loving. It's fantasy, separate from reality.

If she has only glimpsed the potential from role-playing, it will add a fresh, new element to your experience every time your fictional back story changes. However, it shouldn't always be about role-playing. Sometimes, you just need to make love to your lover.

Viagra

I could do this section in two words. "Hell, yea." If you can afford to use Viagra (Sildenafil), then you should.

It'll keep you functioning up to 10-20 minutes after you thought you finished. You never know when she'll want more. It'll help you rise to the challenge.

Oxytocin

I have already mentioned this hormone, but there's enough to get its own subheading.

Psychology Today says: "Oxytocin is a powerful hormone…it influences social interactions and sexual reproduction. It is known for playing a role in behavior from maternal attachment to…orgasm."

Oxytocin is instrumental in all pair bonding and is stimulated significantly during sex, birth, and breastfeeding.

It is responsible for eliciting infatuation. Oxytocin levels increase with touch and have earned the title of "the love hormone."

It was my hormone doctor who told me that cannabis also releases this hormone in copious amounts, which is good because I am a legal participant in my State's medicinal marijuana program.

The G-Spot

I won't keep you in suspense; I have read that it's a myth, but I found more evidence that it's not.

A woman's vagina has a clitoris covered by a layer of skin or hood. This is the area that is known for producing orgasms when stimulated.

The G-Spot is right behind the clitoris, inside the vagina. Using two fingers and a come-hither motion inside her will stimulate the area and cause this bundle of nerves to swell.

When aroused, it swells closer to the surface. Let her feel a G-spot orgasm. Mix a light pounding sensation on her pelvis with your palm in with other movements inside. I'm told the orgasm is distinctly different.

The perceptions each gender hold about sex are growing more similar. Women are having a sexual renaissance. Girls are aggressive about what they want more now than any time I've known.

Women are objectified throughout the world. It's a demotion from the social status of an attractive female to that of an object. Men don't see you, only what you can do for them.

They contribute to their own problem by using seduction as a technique for getting what they want. I don't see it being truly equal. It's not a level playing field.

Appearance is not as crucial to women as men believe. Don't misinterpret me. They're going to be more interactive if they find you attractive.

For me, a genuinely happy woman has an enthusiastic, even daring personality. She is easy-going and helps me see beauty in places men overlook.

Can you look past flaws or extra pounds? According to a recent poll, women place about thirty-four percent of their attraction on appearance.

Chapter Seven: Combining Finances

I would be remiss if I didn't mention one of the leading reasons for failed marriages. I know the chapter title didn't leave much suspense, but it's money, who makes it, and where it goes.

If you've been in a committed relationship, the law of attraction suggests you share a fair number of interests.

Your chosen profession needs to accommodate your economic obligations, but that's not where it should end. Ideally, you would earn enough to have disposable income, or the money left after expenses.

When work is something you would do for free, you never really work a day in your life is an adage I bet most of you have heard.

If it provides you a sufficient measure of satisfaction and compensation, it's more than a job. You have found your purpose.

I manage our household finances. It's not that my wife is incapable. She has a B.S. in Accounting and has been gainfully employed as the Fiscal Director for two different non-profit agencies for many years.

My family's best interests are mine. There is trust, and I keep it, so money is seldom an issue. My sister and her husband manage money much differently, and it has worked well for them.

He pays his bills with his income, and she pays her expenses with hers'. If they need to borrow money, they also need to repay it.

Whatever works for you, works. Coming to terms with the best way to manage your combined income is a subjective matter. There are characteristics specific to the dynamics of the relationship.

My sister and I have been married collectively for hundreds of years. How we manage money may not work for them. The only wrong way to do it is by not doing it.

Remedy any overdraft deficiencies urgently. NSF fees are charged when you spend more money than you have. Show your surprised face now. You're charged another NSF fee, even when your balance drops below zero due to the bank's first NSF fee.

Credit is more than useful and usually necessary. My system isn't structured, but I pay early and often. I do this with all debt. I rarely even know the contract payment because I pay everything ahead.

Do not fret if you carry a few hundred dollars on a credit card from month to month. Allegedly, it helps improve your credit scores. Just be alert. It gets away from you when you turn your head and look back; you suddenly have a four-digit balance to repay.

Money

Both my wife and I have higher educations. Even so, that doesn't make us impervious to error or adversity. There was a time we relied on Public Welfare. We hovered just inches above the rocky bottom before climbing out. My credit score was about 30 points higher than the lowest possible score, 350.

Now, we have disposable income and excellent credit. We live well, if not in every way, in the ways that matter. We have reason for optimism going into the next stage of our lives.

I will take necessary measures to ensure improved living conditions and expanded resources in our future. I prioritize doing the right thing for the right reason.

This book will inspire those who own it in a way that matters. Money is not evil; it's indifferent. The user decides.

Unexpected?

If you are facing unexpected expenses every month, how is it they remain unexpected? Expect the unexpected, especially when it affects your monthly budget.

Something will always happen for which we didn't plan. We can't predict when something will bring about some hefty expenses all at once, but we can prepare for it.

Open a bank account expressly for non-recurring expenses. I recently had some high costs, and the resulting damage is evident when my FICO Score dropped around forty points. It rebounds, but I wouldn't have qualified for the best credit terms.

Credit Reports

Three independent agencies collect data about your payment habits to formulate your FICO score. It's based on aspects that factor into a formula that becomes your risk assessment as a borrower. The scores range from 300 to 850.

A low FICO score indicates a poor payment history and can cause a denial of creditor disqualify you for the best terms. It's frustrating when the agencies lack consistency. You may discover things in your report that shouldn't be there.

Everyone is entitled to one free credit report a year. Get your report and make sure there isn't anything inaccurate. It's a hassle to get bad debt removed. Good credit will save you thousands of dollars in interest.

It can be a little tricky. I've seen my report, and it listed one reason as "not using enough credit," while another factor was "credit balances too high." We can only do what we can do.

It takes no time to lose your credit status, but forever to rebuild it. I had to write letters, negotiate with collection agents, and settle with creditors, until my score breached 800.

Chapter Nine: Instant Meditation

Marijuana has been unjustly represented to the public. Its legal status has little to do with the substance itself. Ulterior agendas were always involved. It was bundled with hard, addictive drugs like cocaine and heroin.

However, the problem was never really with cannabis. It was guilty-by-association. Comparisons of cannabis with other Schedule II substances show they're not as closely related as an apple is with an apricot.

Uniquely Cannabis

This plant has two genders, male and female, that you can quickly identify. THC and CBD are concentrated in females.

We're finally coming around to the truth about marijuana. It isn't rolling marijuana cigarettes; Now, it's cartridges and vaporizers, edibles, capsules, and concentrates.

A Compatible Tandem

I understand why meditation is popular. It's a wise investment of time. Time is money, and this is a time directly yielded as legal tender for achieving lucidity. It refreshes and recharges.

Cannabis is a shortcut to an optimal state-of-mind that enhances meditation. There are two prominent families of this plant with many hybrids. The strain you choose determines how your mind is altered.

A Sativa-dominant product is said to make you "high." It's most associated with heightened cerebral activity. An Indica-dominant product has a narcotic effect. It gets you "stoned." It's the family of strains used to achieve relaxation. Both work to produce desirable results.

Neuroplasticity

Marijuana incites a process called neuroplasticity. It's defined as "the nervous system's capacity to develop new neuronal connections." In other words, using your mind to think is like resistance training; it grows to meet the demand.

Research has proven that older mice have improved brain activities when given cannabis. There were significant variances between them and the control group.

Once you realize nothing has actually changed except you, the need to remedy fades, and you can enjoy the altered state. When you feel good, you lose your false sense of urgency.

Mainstream culture is growing in favor of this substance because it's safer than alcohol and releases hormones like Endorphins and Oxytocin.

An entire generation carries a tainted impression of Cannabis. It was misrepresented in Public Service Announcements that started airing at the dawn of television. Viewers took anything on TV as pure gospel.

The taboo attached to marijuana originated from a campaign funded by William Randolph Hearst to protect his interests in timber.

In those days, there were no disclaimers or truth-in-advertising regulations. They stated it like fact; Cannabis is an evil substance and may cause episodic psychotic rage. It's ridiculous, but it made a lasting impression.

Its legal status created a stereotype of a cannabis user. We tend to live up to the labels we're given. So, they became a stoner, but it doesn't cause any decline in your mental faculties. The opposite is more likely.

We have moments of clarity under the influence that are just as real the next day. My wife believes she is smarter and more efficient using just a little.

Marijuana carried the burden of blame but had a silent partner in alleged crimes. In online reports, prior health issues and alcohol abuse were the primary factors in health problems and as a gateway to other numbing analgesics.

Weed isn't used to self-medicate. You can only get so high, and then you are wasting your supply. Alcohol is available in unlimited quantities but consumed with tragic results.

No one threatens disassociation because someone habitually uses cannabis. It wears off in a couple of hours. Whereas alcohol is the most common reason for professional interventions. Alcohol isn't usually merciful enough to kill you early and in one night.

It takes small bites from you and makes you watch the people you love drift away. The relentless nature of addiction extends your misery and robs you of everything you love in life.

Intoxication has stages that begin with congeniality, arcs with anger, sometimes violence, and end with sadness.

You still have sorrow, embarrassment, and remorse to look forward to tomorrow. Did I leave out "hangover?" That feeling the next day when you wake up and feel like shaving your tongue.

Alcohol is more likely to cause a blind rage, while cannabis impedes it. Marijuana helps relieve depression, moderate physical pain, and on goes the list.

Side-effects

Over-the-counter medications use a disclaimer to protect themselves from any liability caused by negative side-effects.

Marijuana is a drug. Like any drug, it commands respect. A report claims high doses will wreak havoc on your emotions, cause fragmentary thoughts, paranoia, panic attacks, hallucinations, and vertigo.

Just as beauty is in the beholder's eyes, the effects of THC are manifested mainly from our beliefs. It's implied that exceptions exist for everything.

A person can consume enough to make them disoriented. This is symptomatic of *toxic psychosis,* a rare condition where you do not know who or where you are, and time becomes immeasurable to you. I had to dig deep before I found this hazard.

Marijuana, Endorphins, and Oxytocin

Cannabis elicits creative thought, causes the release of Oxytocin, and is all-natural. While they can extract from the plant, it's not altered. It's all-natural.

My doctor put me on my State's medicinal marijuana program. It was a day of which I dreamt. I have many new ways of ingesting it that are much less harsh than the old ways.

Researchers found that brain activity was more active in older mice from the use of cannabis than their counterparts who didn't ingest the substance.

There was a big difference between the two groups. If marijuana incites mice to use more of their minds, what is that likely to mean for humans?

The Pros of using this substance would take a while to assemble. The cons include an increased heart rate, bloodshot eyes, dilated pupils, and often an increased appetite ("the munchies").

It's possible that it has a different impact on me for various reasons, but mostly how it affects my confidence. I have been researching intuition and discovered some amazing facts. Now, I am trying to incorporate using intuition and my philosophy, and they have been merged.

One Day Soon

We'll all have the right to use cannabis legally someday because they can't go back now. Its inconsistent legal status between States is fueling drug-traffic with a potent, government-engineered product.

Prohibition was a bust. It created crime and made alcohol even more desirable. People who didn't drink would start. It's easy to get caught up with *forbidden fruit syndrome*, or the desire to have that from which you are restricted.

In a union, some things shouldn't vary from each state. We may as well be Europe. I live in a state where I'm prescribed medicinal marijuana by a doctor for pain; in Colorado and other states, it's sold recreationally. In contrast, other states keep their status illegal. No one sees the conflict here?

Cannabis loves a peaceful world and has a significant role in helping quiet negative thinking and behavior. Marijuana turns away rage and compels you away from anger and violence.

Dedication

I can't name everyone who influenced this book. The 3,500 readers who commented on my blog article get credit for the book's existence.

There are people I'm yet to meet that will contribute more or less than I can estimate. I'm sure I will owe my gratitude to the editor, who organizes content for enhanced fluency.

This book is different than the fiction I've written. It has a higher worth than anything with entertainment value only.

My happy life will continue by teaching others. Your happiness is my success, our success.

The approach to fitness is intuition-based. It's like fat-burning meditation. There's nothing to pin on your wall. Form habits that are specific to you because this is NOT more of the same.